The 4/14 Window

Raising Up a New Generation to Transform the World

Luis Bush

Contents

Foreword by *Wess Stafford*. v
Introduction. ix

The Opportunity: Understanding the 4/14 Window. 1
    The Intersection of the 10/40 Window and the 4/14 Window 1
    Geographical Challenges. 2
    4/14ers in the Bible. 5
    Vulnerability in the 4/14 Window 8
    4/14ers Around the World 9
    The Modern Context of the 4/14ers 10
    Questions to Ponder. 11

**The Challenge, Part 1: Maximizing the
Transformational Impact of 4/14ers**. 15
    Spiritual Challenge. 17
    Mental/Cognitive Challenge 21
    Physical/Health Challenge. 27
    Economic Challenge. 31

The Challenge, Part 2: Maximizing Transformational Impact 37
    Relational Challenge 37
    Social Challenge. 40
    Ministry Challenge. 46

Holistic Approach to Transformational Development 53
    ConneXions Model for Leadership Development 59

Epilogue: Raising Up a New Generation to Transform Our World 67
About Compassion International 69
Endnotes 71

Foreword

Proverbs 31:8 says, "Speak up for those who cannot speak for themselves." In this book, you will hear a voice that speaks loud and clear for the voiceless, a population that makes up nearly half the world: children.

Christian missions strategist Luis Bush coined the phrase "the 10/40 Window," a concept that has fueled the passion of missions efforts for 15 years. His vision awakened the church to the need to strategically focus ministry on the expanse of the globe that is home to the largest unreached people groups.

Now, Luis will convince you there is an even more strategic target—a window within that window. The vast majority of people who make the

decision to become Christian do so while they are children, between the ages of 4 and 14. This "4/14 Window" is the bull's-eye, the very heart of the harvest.

The dynamic insight of the 4/14 Window demands a significant paradigm shift in missiology thinking. It has been said that "the poor are the lost, and the lost are the poor." The majority of the world's poor live in the 10/40 Window, the poorest countries are the least evangelized, and the poorest of the poor are children—the 4/14 Window. Not only are children the most receptive group to the gospel, they are uniquely positioned to be a powerful kingdom force—even today, as children. And with their whole lives ahead of them to live out and share their faith, they also have time to be long-term agents of change.

Every major movement in history has grasped the need to target the next generation in order to advance its agenda and secure its legacy into the future. Political movements (like Nazism and Communism) trained legions of children with the goal of carrying their agenda beyond the lifetimes of their founders. World religions have done the same with the

systematic indoctrination of their young—even the Taliban places great emphasis on recruiting children. Nebuchadnezzar, in his conquest of Israel, poured his efforts into shaping the future by seeking to influence children like Daniel, Shadrach, Meshach, and Abednego. It seems that, historically, the Christian evangelical movement is one of the few that has allowed children to remain a second-rate mandate—the Great Omission in the Great Commission.

Man's worst sins of *commission* ultimately devastate most severely our smallest citizens. But it is the even more devastating sins of *omission* by the church that are addressed in this powerful book. Few missions organizations invest more than 10% of their budgets in the evangelism and discipleship of children. Churches do only slightly better, typically making budget allocations of 15%, even though every other person in their buildings is a child. We will not bring in the harvest doing more of the same.

Luis Bush calls the Christian community to even greater focus in recognizing the critical value of the 4/14 Window within the 10/40 Window. At the core of this call is the need for a Great Awakening, part two—a transformed worldview that understands that when it comes to children, we must envision beyond our typical 3-year plans to generational 30-year plans. If we will set our ministry sights on children at this watershed moment, the next century of missions will be revolutionized.

The kingdom values of our God are juxtaposed with those of the kingdom of this world in almost every way. In His kingdom, the last are first, the weak are strong, the poor are rich, and—may God grant you the epiphany through this book—the little are big. Those of us who have given our lives to championing the importance of children stand in grateful appreciation for this profound and crucial message from Luis Bush. May God inspire you to join us in His battle for the little ones!

Dr. Wess Stafford
President, Compassion International
Author of *Too Small to Ignore: Why Children Are the Next Big Thing*

Introduction

You have established a stronghold from the mouths of
children . . . to silence the enemy and the avenger.

Psalm 8:2 (HCSB)

At the end of the previous century, I wrote a pamphlet titled *The 10/40 Window: Getting to the Core of the Core.*[1] In this new century, I am urging a new missional focus: the 4/14 Window. Although in a different sense, it too can be called "the core of the core." The 10/40 Window—a term I coined to refer to the regions between 10 and 40 degrees north latitude that contain the world's largest population of non-Christians[2] —referenced a geographic frame. The 4/14 Window describes a demographic season of life comprising the years between ages 4 and 14.

The term "4/14 Window" was introduced at a conference at

Compassion International in Colorado Springs and was published by
Compassion program director Dan Brewster in 1996. The supporting data
was based on research by Bryant Myers, who showed that "85% of those
who become Christians do so between the ages of 4 and 14."[3]

This book is an urgent appeal to consider the strategic importance
and potential of the 1.2 billion children and youth in the 4/14 Window.
It is a plea to open our hearts and minds to the idea of reaching and
raising up a new generation from within this vast group—a generation
that can experience personal transformation and, as a result, become
agents for global transformation. My vision and hope are to maximize
their impact while they are young and to equip them for continuing impact
throughout their lives. I invite you to join with me and many others who
are committed to fulfilling this vision and realizing this hope.

To maximize the transformational impact of children and youth
in the 4/14 Window, we must address the spiritual, mental, physical,
relational, economic, and social issues they face. We must also confront
their "ministry poverty," by which I mean the scarcity of opportunities to
exercise their gifts and reach their potential in ways that honor God and
advance His kingdom.

It is crucial that missions efforts be reprioritized and redirected
toward the 4/14 age group worldwide. This requires that we become
acutely aware of what is taking place in their lives. We must also try to
understand their natures and discern the essential means of nurturing
them in their unique cultural and socioeconomic settings. Only then will
we be able to reach them, shape them, and raise them up to transform
the world.

As a start, this book presents an overview of the seminal needs,
basic nature, and untapped potential of children in the 4/14 Window. It
also addresses the very real opposition and obstacles
to equipping them as a transformational
generation. We must not be defeated by the
opposition or deterred by the obstacles.
And as we engage in strategic global
thinking in response to God's call
to catalytic action, we must do so
within a biblical framework.

The meaning and implications of a world-transforming mission are rooted in the Word of God. In the New Testament, the Bible uses the Greek word *metamorphoo* to describe transformation. *Metamorphoo* is made up of two words: *meta* meaning "change" and *morphoo* meaning "form." In the natural realm, *metamorphoo* describes the process by which a young caterpillar morphs into a beautifully mature adult butterfly. In the Bible, the term is used to describe the transfiguration of Jesus when His outward appearance changed: He became radiant, and His clothes became intensely white (Mark 9:2-3).

Transformation results in a greater likeness to God's nature and a greater adherence to His will for the human race. *Metamorphoo* is used in 2 Corinthians 3:18 to describe this process: "Being transformed into the same image from one degree of glory to another. For this comes from the Lord who is the Spirit." It is clear that transformation comes from the Lord, for it is rooted in His nature and is an expression of His character.

Scripture also makes it absolutely clear that the transformational mission of God involves bringing together all things under the headship of Christ through the church, which is His body (Ephesians 1:9-10). The church is the fullness of Christ on earth, who fills all in all (Ephesians 1:22-23), with the result that all things are to be reconciled and aligned to Him (Colossians 1:20). The members of the body of Christ—including children and youth in the 4/14 Window—are God's agents of transformation under His headship. Every Christ follower in every community and nation—even children and youth—is called to involvement in His transformational mission.

When approaching this bold initiative, we do well to adopt the watchwords "transformed and always transforming." This simple phrase reminds us that transformation is a process that will not be fully realized until Jesus comes again. We are co-laborers with Christ under His headship, collaborating in His transformational mission to raise up a new generation from the 4/14 Window to change the world.

Such global transformation will only take place as God's people are individually remade through the renewing of our minds (Romans 12:1-2). Only then will we discover the good and perfect will of God. This will be our "spiritual worship" and will result in our being engaged in God's mission.

May God renew our minds through His Word, and may the vision presented in this book challenge us to be His change agents to transform the world as we know it for the glory of Christ.

Luis Bush

The Opportunity:
Understanding the 4/14 Window

In human development, there is no more critical period than the decade encompassed by the 4/14 Window. It is a profoundly formative period when perspectives are shaped either positively or negatively and when a view of one's own significance (or lack thereof) is formulated. The needs and potential of this age group should inspire a purposeful response by those charged today with transforming tomorrow's world. It is a call to "turn the hearts of fathers to their children and the hearts of children to their fathers" (Malachi 4:6).

According to *Global Trends 2025: A World Transformed,* by the year 2025, we can expect more cultural and religious clashes, more trouble spots, and the enduring consequences of a "global financial tsunami." The purpose of this November 2008 report, prepared by hundreds of renowned international social scientists, was "to stimulate strategic thinking about the future by identifying key trends, the factors that drive them, where they seem to be headed, and how they might interact."[4] The ideas, values, and cultural norms that shape the future of societies are forged during the 4/14 Window.

This book is more than an effort to "stimulate strategic thinking." It is a *Christian call to action.* We must think strategically, of course, but it is imperative that we also act decisively to reach, protect, inspire, and equip this generation of 4/14ers to transform the world. If we don't, an entire generation could be lost.

The Intersection of the 10/40 Window
and the 4/14 Window

The 10/40 Window represents the primary geographic challenge to the church of the 21st century in that it is the geographical location in which each of *five key challenges* are indisputably and significantly more prominent. (See sidebar below.)[5]

Sixteen years into a worldwide missions emphasis on the 10/40 Window, there are encouraging indicators that this region has been highly responsive to the gospel (see map at right). The annual growth rate of Christ followers inside the 10/40 Window was almost twice that of those outside the Window.[6] Christ followers in 10/40 Window nations increased from 2.5% of the population in 1990 to 4.7% in 2005. The general population grew at only 1.5% annually, while the population of Christ followers grew at an amazing 5.4% per year![7]

Correlate these statistics with the fact that almost 70% of the world's

---

Geographical Challenges

The Urban Challenge: The people of the 21st century will live in an urban world for the first time. Currently 50% of the world lives in an urban setting. By the end of the 21st century 80% of the world will be urbanized. The expanding slums and shantytowns of the world's cities are already populated by one billion people. Nearly 40% of the developing world live in these dilapidated dwellings. This century will necessitate pioneer missionaries who will give their lives for the city.

The Social Challenge: Social responsibility has been recognized and affirmed in the last 25 years as an essential component of Christ's Great Commission. An estimated 10 million children suffer forced prostitution. Malnutrition kills 35,000 children under five every day. The number of street children has grown to 100 million. These facts make the world's children an epicenter of Christian social responsibility. Several other great social concerns afflict us as we enter the 21st century. AIDS in Africa has grown to alarming proportions with millions of adults infected and millions of children orphaned in the aftermath. The next decade will result in tens of millions of additional AIDS orphans. Drug addiction, along with the illegal, global drug manufacturing and trading industry, strangles the people in cities and countries today. Infectious diseases like tuberculosis and malaria continue to slaughter millions.

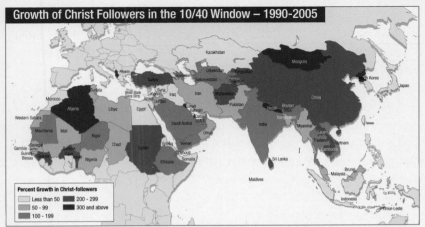

Growth of Christ Followers in the 10/40 Window – 1990-2005

Percent Growth in Christ-followers
- Less than 50
- 50 - 99
- 100 - 199
- 200 - 299
- 300 and above

NOTE: The dramatic % change in some counties is partially attributed to the low evangelical population in 1990: Mongolia (552), North Korea (104,960), Nepal (131,605), Algeria (5,038), Kuwait (2,452), Qatar (2,336), Afghanistan (2,696), Albania (1,154), Turkey (8,145), Kyrgyzstan (9,288), and Saudi Arabia (87,000)

Sources: Patrick Johnstone – data prepared for two upcoming publications; United Nations   Map by Global Mapping International, Jan. 2009

The People Challenge: More than 1000 peoples are still without a viable indigenous church planting movement in their midst with sufficient strength, resources, and commitment to sustain and ensure the continuous multiplication of churches. Various strategic ministries need to be strengthened for this discipling process to be effective and lasting. More research, church planting efforts, literature production, *Jesus Film* distribution, Scripture translation, and radio ministries are required.

The Ideological Challenge: The Islamic worldview presents a substantive ideological challenge with social and legal systems that make it nearly impossible for a Muslim to become a Christian. Then there is the growth of "fundamentalist" terrorism. The pluralism of Hindus and the atheism of Buddhists require innovative approaches. Other ideological challenges are presented by the Baha'i, the Sikhs, the Jains, and animists. Worst of all, nominal Christians have settled for a form of godliness with no power.

The Spiritual Challenge: We have been involved in spiritual warfare ever since Satan wrested control of the world. We will constantly face the two equally dangerous challenges of either "underemphasis" on the spiritual nature of the conflict or a "preoccupation" with the enemy. Prayer makes a profound difference in world evangelization. Global networks of prayer have been raised up to meet this challenge.

(From Patrick Johnstone, *The Church Is Bigger Than You Think*, [Scotland: Christian Focus Publications, 1998].)

4-to-14 year olds (833,378,750 as of 2010) live in the 10/40 Window, and we can see the intersection of the 10/40 and 4/14 Windows.[8] The 10/40 Window is the geographical area with the greatest need and opportunity. The 4/14 Window is the demographic group that is the most open and receptive to every form of spiritual and developmental input.

The compelling conclusion is that our missional efforts should be refocused on the 4/14 Window within the 10/40 Window. We should be targeting the most receptive persons in the most responsive areas. In so doing we are also recognizing the importance of children and youth in God's work of transforming the world.

Jesus warned His disciples:

> Truly, I say to you, unless you turn and become like children, you will never enter the kingdom of heaven. Whoever humbles himself like this child is the greatest in the kingdom of heaven.

Whoever receives one such child in my name receives me, but whoever causes one of these little ones who believe in me to sin, it would be better for him to have a great millstone fastened around his neck and to be drowned in the depth of the sea. (Mathew 18:3-6)

Have we really listened to this teaching about the place of children in the kingdom of God? It contains three truths: First, children model the essence of saving faith and discipleship. Becoming like them is required in order to "enter the kingdom of heaven." Second, to "welcome a child"—that is, to accept, love, value, and respect a child—is to welcome Christ Himself! Finally, as Jesus made very clear, whoever neglects, abuses, hinders, or turns away a child from faith will face God's severe judgment.

Christ is the King of the kingdom, and the faith of a child is the model for all who would enter and live under the rule of King Jesus. The gospel elevates children to a place of honor in the kingdom and acknowledges their moral agency. Children are addressed as responsible members of the family of God, as those who are "in the Lord" (Ephesians 6:1).

4/14ers in the Bible

Children and youth as agents of God's work is not a new concept. In both the Old and the New Testaments we frequently see God using children and young people to transform their world.

Throughout Scripture we see God entrusting special truths to children or using them as His special messengers or instruments. Wess Stafford, president of Compassion International, often says that when God has something *really* important to do, something that He couldn't entrust to adults, He uses children. Stafford continues, "God seems to pause, rub his hands together, smile warmly, and say, 'I need someone really powerful for this task. I know . . . I'll use a child.'"[9]

This is illustrated numerous times in the Bible. One example is the Old Testament story of Naaman, an army commander who suffered from leprosy, then an incurable disease. A young Israelite girl who served Naaman's wife told her mistress about Elisha, a prophet of God who could help in seemingly helpless situations (2 Kings 5:2). The wife told her husband, and following the young girl's suggestion, Naaman went to Elisha and was miraculously cured. But beyond his physical healing,

Naaman experienced a spiritual revelation: "Behold, I know that there is no God in all the earth but in Israel" (2 Kings 5:15). The intervention of a child had resulted in that all-important "now I know" realization.[10] Today, as in ages past, children and young people are vessels in God's hands, pointing the way to faith when adults have become corrupt, distracted, or deaf to His calling.

The cast of 4/14ers in the Bible includes some fascinating individuals: *Samuel* was the child through whom God delivered a needful but difficult message to the high priest, Eli. Samuel's sensitivity to God's leading and his ready obedience were exemplary (1 Samuel 3).

David was only a youth when God chose and began to use him. David was the youngest of eight brothers, so his own father did not even consider him when Samuel came seeking God's choice to be Israel's next king. And while he was probably still a teenager, David slew the giant Goliath and inspired his nation to rout their enemies, the dreaded Philistines (1 Samuel 17).

Josiah was a boy-king through whom God reformed the religious and social state of his people (2 Kings 22). Josiah was a mere eight years old when he began his righteous rule. He later made dramatic reforms as a teenager and a young man (2 Chronicles 34).

Esther was an orphan who while probably in her teens, became a queen whom God used to save the Jewish people from annihilation (Esther 2).

Timothy had biblical faith from childhood, passed along from his grandmother Lois and his mother, Eunice, and later matured through Paul's instruction (2 Timothy 1:5; 2:2; 3:14-15). So great was Paul's confidence in Timothy that he entrusted the churches to Timothy's pastoral care.

"It is not just that these people happened to be children," writes Keith White, founder and director of the Child Theology Movement, "but that some of the most significant acts and revelations of God were through these children. Their faith and actions are critically important in the unfolding and outworking of God's purposes."[11]

The New Testament provides only brief accounts of Jesus' own childhood, but the examples given are significant. Soon after she learned she was pregnant with the holy child, Mary visited her cousin Elizabeth to share the amazing news. Elizabeth was also expecting her first child—a son who would become the great prophet John the Baptist. "When

Elizabeth heard the greeting of Mary, the baby leaped in her womb. And Elizabeth was filled with the Holy Spirit" (Luke 1:41). Some months later Mary gave birth to Jesus in a Bethlehem stable. A short time after that, Jesus was taken by His parents to Egypt in order to escape Herod's murderous rampage.

When Jesus and His parents returned from Egypt, they settled in the village of Nazareth. In that obscure place, Jesus "grew and became strong, filled with wisdom. And the favor of God was upon him" (Luke 2:40). At age 12, Jesus accompanied His family on a journey to Jerusalem for the Passover festival. He went to the temple, where Mary and Joseph found Him "sitting among the teachers, listening to them and asking them questions. And all who heard him were amazed at his understanding and his answers" (Luke 2:42-47). Upon the family's return to Nazareth, Jesus was obedient to them and "increased in wisdom and stature and in favor with God and man" (Luke 2:52).

During His three years of public ministry, Jesus observed the characteristics of children and referred to them as examples to adult

believers. Noting the value of childlike humility, He said, "Whoever humbles himself like this child is the greatest in the kingdom of heaven" (Matthew 18:4). Contrary to the preconceived notions of many adults, children everywhere—just like Jesus when He was a child—can grasp spiritual truths easily. They can sense the guilt of sin,[12] understand their need for a Savior, and grasp the significance of faith. In Charles Spurgeon's words, "A child of five, if properly instructed, can truly believe and be regenerated as much as any adult."[13]

"But Jesus, knowing the reasoning of their hearts, took a child and put him by his side and said to them, 'Whoever receives this child in my name receives me, and whoever receives me receives him who sent me. For he who is least among you all is the one who is great'" (Luke 9:47-48).

Vulnerability in the 4/14 Window

The world's 4/14ers present us with several pressing realities. These years represent a "season of awakening" in which a person's understanding of life emerges and one's conscience is awakened to judge right from wrong. But the life circumstances of today's typical 4/14er are a cross between a minefield and an obstacle course.

A disturbing number of 4/14ers in the 10/40 Window are condemned to a life of serfdom, brutal labor, sexual exploitation, spiritual oppression, and emotional abuse. As maturing teenagers, most of them quickly leave behind parents' supervision. When formal schooling ends, they either enter the workforce to make ends meet or further their education in an environment fraught with the dangers of secular ideology and materialism.

Parents and older siblings serve as the most potent and positive influences for many 4/14ers. But sadly, for many others, parents are negligent and siblings are morally damaging. This is especially true when those older brothers and sisters are themselves adversely influenced by today's toxic youth cultures.

Although challenges and pitfalls abound, and the pessimism of many adults is amply warranted, the potential of 4/14ers and the possibilites available to them are astonishing. The tendency for many adults is to ignore or dismiss the potential of 4/14ers or to view them as a nagging problem to be endured. The majority of adults fail to grasp the inestimable value of these young lives made in the image of God. Most significantly, adults fail to recognize that most people who decide to follow Christ do so during the critical years between the ages of 4 and 14.

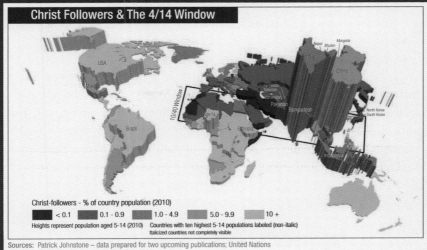

Christ Followers & The 4/14 Window

Christ-followers - % of country population (2010)

< 0.1   0.1 - 0.9   1.0 - 4.9   5.0 - 9.9   10 +

Heights represent population aged 5-14 (2010)   Countries with ten highest 5-14 populations labeled (non-italic)
Italicized countries not completely visible

Sources: Patrick Johnstone – data prepared for two upcoming publications; United Nations
Map by Global Mapping International, Jan. 2009

4/14ers Around the World

A country-by-country comparison of the nations with the most 4/14ers is revealing. India, with almost 20% fewer people than China, has over 30% more children and youth.[14] This is largely due to China's controversial "one child" policy. Nigeria and Indonesia, with half the population of the U.S., actually have more children and young teens in absolute numbers.

The greatest population growth of 4/14ers by far is taking place in the least developed and most conflicted countries of the world. The continent of Africa and countries like Gaza, Afghanistan, Pakistan, and most of the Middle East have 40 to 50% of their populations under 15 years of age.[15] Contrast this with the countries with the lowest percentage of persons under age 15: Italy (13.8%), Japan (14.3%), and Germany (14.4%).[16]

From a missions standpoint our interest in 4/14ers is not only because they are the most receptive but also because, as we have shown, they are often the most effective agents for mission. Jesus obviously understood their worth: "I thank you Father, Lord of heaven and earth, that you have hidden these things from the wise and understanding and revealed them to little children; yes, Father, for such was your gracious will" (Matthew 11:25-26).

In a three-year project called *The Child in Law, Religion and Society*, researchers examined the so-called mystery of the child. Their final report urges readers to reject the prevalent view that a child is a problem to be controlled. Instead, the authors contend, adults ought to nurture wonder in children while seeking their own "childlikeness," or "childness." They warn against the fallacy of reductionism—the philosophy that attempts to reduce a complex system to the sum of its parts. In this case, reductionism endeavors to categorize a child through various problematic elements. For example, the incidence of delinquency, abuse, or autism. Some reductionists go so far as to define a child as "the sum of neuron firings in the brain," or "nothing but a victim of original sin."[17] Such thinking demeans the wondrous, mysterious nature of childhood.

The Modern Context of the 4/14ers

The 4/14ers (and their older siblings) are called the Internet Generation because the Net is their primary influencer. While their parents are digital immigrants, the world's children and young people are digitally native. They are less defined by geography than by technology.

It is true that there are still parts of the world where the Internet does not yet have a major culture-shaping role due to a lack of accessibility. However, with the shrinking of the global village, more and more young people in remote areas are becoming connected and correspondingly influenced by the culture of Western materialism and hedonism.

Today's children and young people have been given labels such as "Digital Kids," "Millennials," or "Mosaics." These tags suggest that today's kids are vastly different in culture and worldview from the Baby Boomers. They are living in a postmodern age in which the spirit of deconstructionism is eroding their values, affecting their self-identity, and changing their views of the home, school, and society.[18]

Today's young people are "Facebookers," "YouTubers," and "Twitterers" who do not think twice about sharing their opinions online with strangers whom they call friends. Technology is a powerful vehicle for change, but it is also a powerful poison that can bring destruction. This generation wants their opinions heard, and they want to make a difference. They are creative and open with their feelings.[19]

The 4/14ers are riding a technological wave into the future. More than any previous generation, they are plugged in 24/7, with a world of communication and information at their fingertips. "The youth of today, due to the strong influence of technology in their everyday lives, are constantly confronted with the problem of self-definition. To most adolescents, technologies such as mobile phones are implicated in the production of individuality and personhood."[20]

Traditional values face unprecedented challenges in the digital world. The Internet provides youth the world over with instant access to a wide variety of lifestyles and "McWorld" values. The technological culture has a global reach, replacing even long-held values. India exemplifies this global youth-culture phenomenon. It is a nation where communication technology has produced dramatic changes resulting in a drastic decline in traditional values. The information age is widening social distances there, weakening family ties, and changing the child-parent relationship.

The World Values Survey findings[21] accentuate the conclusion that intergenerational changes are taking place in basic values related to politics, economics, religion, gender roles, family, and sexual norms. The values of the younger generation consistently differ from those prevailing among older generations and are transforming social, economic, and political life—in some cases displacing thousands of years of tradition in the span of a single generation.

There is much that is frightening and disheartening in the information explosion and "flattening" of this "brave new world". As uncomfortable as we in the older generations might be with the Internet culture, it is undeniable that the 4/14ers are very much at home there and will be even more so as it expands at an unprecedented pace. However, we must understand and accept that this very connectedness, instant information access, and sharing are part of the great potential of the 4/14ers to transform their world.

Questions to Ponder

The Bible provides some clear, compelling answers to these important questions:

Want to enter God's kingdom?
   Become like little children.
Want to be great in God's eyes?
   Become like little children.
Want to let Jesus know you welcome Him?
   Welcome little children.

Want to avoid judgment at God's hand?
Don't lead little children astray.
Want to identify with God's plans?
Don't belittle or despise little children.
Want to follow Jesus' example?
Love, pray for, accept, be with, and bless little children.[22]

The New Testament confirms the high regard Jesus had for children. There were many incidents involving children in His life: the boy who offered Jesus the loaves and fishes (John 6); the son of the widow of Nain (Luke 7:11-17); the daughter of the Canaanite woman (Matthew 15:22), just to list a few examples. Although we may not know their names, their presence in the biblical record confirms their significance to Jesus. Though it is often overlooked, we cannot deny the prominent role of children in Christ's life and ministry.[23]

Indeed, throughout the Bible we see God's very high regard for their ability to understand the faith and to participate in His redemptive activities. Young people are encouraged to influence their communities by maintaining personal purity, by obeying God's Word (Psalm 119:9), by being exemplary in their speech, love, and faith (1 Timothy 4:12), and by pursuing godly virtues (2 Timothy 2:22). In fact, the conduct and moral standards for children as described in the Bible differ very little from those outlined for adults.[24]

To Jesus, children were living examples of what the kingdom was all about. "Truly, I say to you, whoever does not receive the kingdom of God like a child shall not enter it" (Mark 10:15). It was Jesus who commended children over and over as meaning makers, spiritual pilgrims, and active agents with a God-given ministry on earth.

Keith White asks, "What if we miss the whole idea of doing theology, missions, and church simply because we, as adults, have misheard or neglected God's revealed teaching about children and childhood?"[25]

Why did God use children to teach kingdom truths? Who was Jesus' audience, if not adults?

It is imperative that we see children and young people as a strategic force that can transform a generation and change the world. Jesus said, "To such [children] belongs the kingdom of God" (Luke 18:16). And yet from His time to the present day, the church has often underestimated the value and potential of children. Time and again we have failed to

effectively and strategically reach them. The challenge before us is to raise up today's 4/14ers . . .

- to experience the abundant life Jesus promised (John 10:10b);

- to be freed from spiritual, mental, physical, relational, economic, and social poverty;

- to harness their immense potential; and

- to change the world.

The Challenge, Part 1: Maximizing the Transformational Impact of 4/14ers

Any sensible parent knows the childhood years are formative. Anyone who has been a child knows it too! Our brains are 90% formed before we reach the age of three,[26] and 85% of our adult personality is formed by the time we reach six years of age. There is substantial truth in the Jesuits' refrain, "Show me a child when he is seven, and I'll show you the man." A biblical proverb attributed to King Solomon, the wisest man who ever lived, instructs us, "Train up a child in the way he should go; even when he is old he will not depart from it" (Proverbs 22:6). In light of this truth, our task is to "train up" the 4/14 generation in the way they should go, so that as they grow older, they can be used by God to transform the world.

This is a multifaceted challenge, and it can only be met with a

holistic approach. When raising up the 4/14 generation for transformational impact, we must address their physical needs (especially of those in poverty), their intellectual needs, and all the relational, social, and spiritual dimensions of their lives. We must embrace the whole person, endeavoring to see 4/14ers as God sees them.

When relating to children who live in impoverished conditions, we must look beyond the lack of assets and advantages and see the complete individual. We must also recognize the cyclical, negative forces at work. Jayakumar Christian, a leader with World Vision in India, describes poverty as a set of disempowering systems that result in ongoing or even intensified poverty.[27]

As the illustration on this page shows, these exploitative systems interact with each other to supplant the role of God in the lives of the poor. This results in the development of absolute structures that oppress people and distort their view of God. Cultural systems legitimize these God complexes and reinforce the distortions. All of these systems are based on deception and lies about who people really are and who God really is. They systematically victimize people who are made in the image of God, exchanging the truth for a lie and causing people to worship and serve created things rather than the Creator (Romans 1:25).

As a result of their marred identities and vocational insecurities, the poor believe that they were born to be oppressed. They also conclude they have nothing to offer, and their negative identities become self-fulfilling prophecies. (The non-poor, on the other hand, often believe they have the right to exploit others and to enjoy the fruits of the poor's

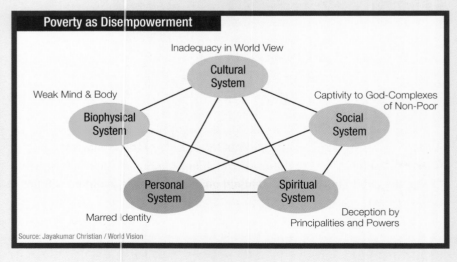

Poverty as Disempowerment

Inadequacy in World View

Cultural System

Weak Mind & Body

Captivity to God-Complexes of Non-Poor

Biophysical System

Social System

Personal System

Spiritual System

Marred Identity

Deception by Principalities and Powers

Source: Jayakumar Christian / World Vision

labor.) As long as these core perspectives remain in effect, a fatalistic mind-set locks the poor into their poverty. What is true of the world's poor is especially true of the children and youth, whose lives are molded and futures are cast during childhood.

The 4/14 Window is the first point of access to reverse the systematic lies of culture and to remake a generation through holistic development. In this chapter and the next, I will examine each of the seven basic challenges in the 4/14 Window: spiritual, mental, physical, economic, relational, social and ministry challenges.

Spiritual Challenge

As noted previously, most people who make a decision to follow Christ will do so before their 15th birthday. In the U.S. nearly 85% of those who make this decision do so between the ages of 4 and 14.[28] During the 20th century, this age group was the largest source of new believers for the American church.

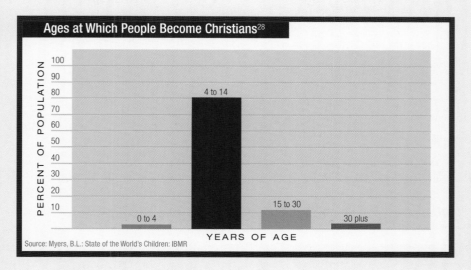

Ages at Which People Become Christians[28]

Source: Myers, B.L.: State of the World's Children: IBMR

In his book *Transforming Your Children into Spiritual Champions*,[29] George Barna presents the results of three years of research that confirm the timeless principle from the Wisdom Literature: "Train up a child in the way he should go; even when he is old he will not depart from it" (Proverbs 22:6).

Barna's research verifies that a person's lifelong behaviors and beliefs are generally developed during childhood and early adolescence. In the case of the overwhelming majority of us, most of our moral and spiritual foundations are in place by age nine. Fundamental perspectives on truth, integrity, meaning, justice, morality, and ethics are formed at this early stage.

In the 4/14 age group, we also see the natural confluence of evangelism and discipleship. Barna observes, "By the age of 13, one's spiritual identity is largely set in place."[30] If we can reach children and youth and disciple them when their life perspectives and worldviews are being shaped, we will set them firmly on a rock that cannot be easily moved.

These statistics reveal a vast spiritual harvest waiting to be reaped. For too long the ministries of most churches, Christian organizations, and mission agencies have focused primarily on adults, with fewer personnel, minimal funds, and limited creativity devoted to children and adolescents. In no way should we abandon the outreach to any age group, but the call of the 4/14 initiative is clear: We must prioritize our efforts to reach the world's largest, most receptive, and most moldable group—the 4/14ers.

However, just because children tend to be receptive to the gospel does not mean that we can be carefree in how we approach them or their parents. Indeed, that heightened receptivity should cause us to be even more cautious and discerning, for the possibility of exploitation or abuse is also heightened.

Admittedly, focusing on the 4/14ers is a challenge more easily met in some nations than in others. Cross-cultural missionaries must study the cultures and the contexts of the adult peoples to whom they minister. The same applies to those who would do "mission work" among children. When ministering to them, the servant of Christ must be wise, sensitive, cautious, discerning, and holistic in reaching out to those in non-Christian settings.

In 2008, the Global Children's Forum (GCF) was formed. The GCF is a partnership of children's ministry agencies operating on a regional or global basis. Its focus is on the strategic need for evangelism and discipleship among the world's two billion children. Its goal is to ensure that every child is given the opportunity to know who Jesus is, what He offers, and how to know Him personally.

The map on the following page provides a vivid picture of the spiritual challenges among the nations. The spiritually neediest places in the world (shown in red) are the places where the 4/14ers have the least opportunity of hearing the gospel.

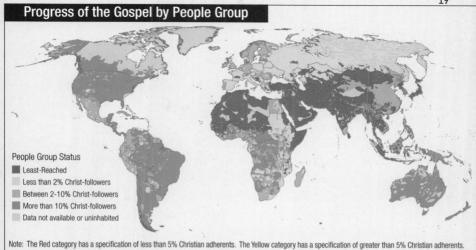

Progress of the Gospel by People Group

People Group Status
- Least-Reached
- Less than 2% Christ-followers
- Between 2-10% Christ-followers
- More than 10% Christ-followers
- Data not available or uninhabited

Note: The Red category has a specification of less than 5% Christian adherents. The Yellow category has a specification of greater than 5% Christian adherents.

Source: Based on the Joshua Project Progress Scale: Joshua Project (Feb. 2008)
Map prepared for 4/14 Window publication and produced by Joshua Project and Global Mapping International

Spiritual Transformation Brings Community Transformation: God at Work Through His People

The heart of transformation is the transformation of the heart. The central need is spiritual in nature. This is clear from God's Word, where He reveals His perfect plan to reverse the effects of the fall on His creation. Spiritual transformation does not only mean the forgiveness of sins; it encompasses all of life, re-created by God. The spiritual transformation of the individual through the power of the gospel provides the platform upon which every sphere of society can be transformed.

By "transformation" I do not mean behavior modification or a striving to make the world a better place. Transformation entails a passionate seeking after God, submitting to His power, and allowing Him to realign every facet of our lives according to His design and plan.

Although God desires to radically change each individual, there is also a communal component to transformation—the body of Christ. This is a community of individuals who have been transformed by the gospel. The body of Christ is the place where societal transformation begins and from which individuals emerge as agents of transformation in their various spheres of influence. This was clearly demonstrated through the work of the body of Christ in the Bihar State of India after a devastating flood.

Model of an Effective Approach to
the Spiritual Challenge

Northern India represents one of the world's greatest spiritual challenges. It has been said that if India is at the core of the 10/40 Window, northern India is at the core of the core, and the state of Bihar is at the core of that core.

In August 2008 Bihar suffered one of the worst floods in its history. A breeched dam on the Kosi River in Nepal unleashed a devastating flood that inundated 15 districts and swept away all in its path. The gushing waters from the dam were 15 kilometers in width. Initial estimates were that 3.1 million people were affected. Tens of thousands died within hours.

The NIEA (New India Evangelistic Association) linked with other regional ministries in a two-month project to meet the acute needs of more than 20,000 people who were left homeless, without shelter, and paralyzed with fear. In addition to relief packets and medical treatment given to tens of thousands, the Agape Relief camp was established to minister to hundreds of displaced children. More than 500 victims stayed in the Agape Relief camp for about two months.

Every evening a team of boys and girls from children's homes run by the ministry went to the camp to sing, pray, and minister to the hurting community. Their songs and testimonies brought comfort, hope, and joy as they sang of the love of Jesus the Savior and prayed for Him to heal the hurting community.

Later on in December 2008, a team of 20 pastors and children visited Bihar's flood-affected Madhepura district and discovered houses, shops, and businesses that were devastated by the deluge. One resident, Mr. Kumar, said, "We have lost all that we earned. When we returned our house was still in about three feet of water. We have to start from scratch...." The team arrived with the *Jesus* video, set up a portable screen, and shared that "the Man of Nazareth" had come to Madhepura this cold Christmas season and that He offered them His love and hope.

A crowd of about 3,500 turned up to see the film and meet the members of the team. Hearts were touched, and many wept when they saw Jesus heal the sick. Heads nodded as Jesus taught the crowds. The people were amazed. Most poignantly, they looked in awe as Jesus calmed the raging waters. This Jesus was one who brought hope and who could even calm the churning seas!

At the close of the meeting, about 90% of the crowd indicated that they wanted to give their lives to Jesus, and more than 800 remained for prayer. The children and missionaries prayed for this new community of Christ followers who had welcomed Jesus into their hearts. In the following weeks, five churches were established in the community. Children have helped to address the spiritual needs of the area by ministering at church services and open-air meetings. In the future, the ministry will focus on the rehabilitation of flood-affected children through the establishment of child-development programs and orphan homes for displaced children.

Villages of Hope

Another example of spiritual transformation is the Village of Hope model. World Help, a U.S.-based relief and development organization, is engaged in a long-term strategy to provide aid and encouragement to children whose extended families simply cannot care for them. By establishing Villages of Hope throughout sub-Saharan Africa, World Help is caring for orphans and unwanted children in small, family-like Homes of Hope.

The organization's Villages of Hope are not compounds to which children are removed; rather, they are located in or near existing villages. The strategy keeps children within their culture and community, utilizing local schools and clinics to provide education and health care for them. Many of the older children receive vocational skills and training. The typical Village of Hope is tightly integrated with its local neighbors, helping not only the children in the home but also many others in the broader community.

The children who live in the Homes of Hope are enveloped within a godly environment that fosters strong communal relationships. They see God's love in action every day and are growing up within their culture rather than being removed from it. The vision is to see hundreds of these hope-filled villages and homes caring for thousands of children whose lives have been turned upside down by HIV/AIDS and other calamities.

Mental/Cognitive Challenge

By the time the typical child reaches age nine, the mental gears are shifted, and he or she begins to use internal cues to either confirm or challenge an existing perspective. As the child grows into adolescence, change becomes more and more difficult. By adulthood, only with great effort or under great influence will a person change existing views and understandings. George Barna notes that "adults essentially carry out the beliefs they embraced when they were young."[31] This view challenges the stages of intellectual development[32] formulated by Jean Piaget and colleagues, contending that one must reach the age of 15 to be capable of adult reasoning.

Every mature society recognizes childhood and adolescence as times to prepare the young for the remainder of their lives. Most often this is done through primary and secondary schools. Educators worldwide understand the critical importance of the 4/14 Window in the correct formation of children; however, despite the efforts of many governments, untold millions of children receive little or no education. This problem of substandard education is exacerbated by other factors, including the disintegration of the family unit, poverty, ill health, poor nutrition, to name but a few. This results in masses of unmotivated, poorly educated men and women, barely capable of earning a meager income. The situation is further complicated for children whose own parents deprive them of an education by forcing them to work in order to help support the family.

The Need for a Transformational Approach to Education

While universal primary and secondary education may be considered a worthy goal, its ultimate effect can sometimes be negative. Unless the teachers and administrators are Christ followers, the worldview that is taught will not transform the minds of the 4/14ers to be able to test and approve what God's will is for them (Romans 12:1-2). A further complication is that childhood education in many countries has been taken away from the jurisdiction of the parents and the church.

Secular education does not enlighten; rather, it dims one's grasp of the "real reality" rooted in the truth of Scripture. It seeks to remove the notion that God exists or that we owe allegiance to a Creator. Naturalistic worldviews and rationalism in secular education have conspired to predispose children against the supernatural and even to despise it. By teaching children a curriculum that robs God of His rightful preeminence, such educational systems are sabotaging the blessing of Jesus, who "came that they may have life and have it abundantly" (John 10:10).

Godless, secular indoctrination is an age-old problem, one that we see described in the Bible. Consider the experience of Daniel and his three friends (Daniel 1). They were only boys, 11 to 14 years old, taken

from their parents and shipped off to pagan Babylon. Their captors even gave them new names—a practice that continues in Christless authoritarian systems to this day. What happened to Daniel and his friends was like the name changes given to local residents on the Korean peninsula at the beginning of the 20th century in the Soviet Union after the Bolshevik Revolution in 1917. The four boys in Babylon were given heathen names to replace their covenantal names associated with the one true God.

The plan was to win them for Babylon, to transform their minds until they were completely captivated by the Babylonian thought forms, worldview, culture, religion, and way of life. But all of their captors' attempts failed miserably. Daniel and his friends did not forget their early God-centered education; they did not lose their faith; they would not be robbed of trust in the one true God.

The Babylonian system of public education, with its goal of a pervasive secularism, reminds us of the government-run educational systems of today. In a pluralistic, secular society, public education is not allowed to teach a Christ-centered worldview. But this can be offset by Christian teachers who serve as salt and light within the system and by Christian parents who train their children to be discerning—to be in the world but not of it.[33] Our task may be to raise Daniels in Babylon.

As we consider the public education systems at the beginning of the 21st century, we must find encouragement from the book of Daniel that God is supreme, that He is in control, that He can be trusted. More than once the worldly king of Babylon, the feared Nebuchadnezzar, was moved to declare about God, "His kingdom is an eternal kingdom, and his dominion endures from generation to generation" (Daniel 4:3b, 34). We can learn from those who have gone before us: from Daniel and his friends, from educators like Saint Augustine, and from others who stayed faithful in pursuit of God's purposes. A transformational approach to education begins with the premise that all truth is God's truth. Augustine's legacy is that it is the duty of the Christian to learn as much as possible about as many things as possible, including scientific inquiry and the pursuit of knowledge and beauty, recognizing that God is the ultimate Source of all truth and beauty. Therefore we encourage parents and their children to be discerning in what they learn, whatever their educational context. They must reject what is anti-Christian, accept and use what is true, and through the gospel transform secular knowledge and culture into serviceable "Egyptian gold" to serve and worship God (Exodus 35:20-29).

The Outcome of the Transformation of the Mind: Transformation of Cultures and Nations

As with Daniel, the renewing or metamorphosis of the mind (Romans 12:1-2) can result in the transformation of the culture. The manifesto of a new, influential school of thought on human progress and nation building is called *Culture Matters: How Values Shape Human Progress* by Samuel P. Huntington and Lawrence E. Harrison.[34]

The far-reaching essays in the book are drawn from a historic symposium sponsored by the Harvard Academy for International and Area Studies. Leading experts address everything from the effect of culture on various nations to its role in shaping gender issues.

These scholars also ponder the question of why, at the beginning of the twenty-first century, the world is more divided than ever between the rich and the poor, between those living in freedom and those under oppression. They conclude that cultural values shape the development of nations and offer an important insight into why some countries and ethnic/religious groups have done better than others, not just in economic terms, but also with respect to democratic institutions and social justice. Former Singaporean prime minister Lee Kuan Yew said, "More than economics, more than politics, a nation's culture will determine its fate."[35] In our world there is no greater example of two nations that share the same family roots yet have two totally different cultures and fates than North and South Korea.

Sister Nations, Separate Cultures

To avoid unfair comparisons, one needs to use an objective measurement. Two such country-transformation indicators are the economic prosperity and the religious freedom of nations.[36]

In 1953, South Korea was the poorest nation in Asia. It is now the 3rd most prosperous country there, ranking 10th in the world. Its citizens live with an incomparably greater freedom of religion than the people of North Korea. In dramatic contrast, after 55 years of dictatorial rule, North Korea remains among the poorest nations in the world. One of the starkest differences between North and South Korea is seen in the education received by their children. In great measure South Korea's educational system has grown out of a worldview fostered by its churches, Christian families, and influential believers. North Korea, however, has shaped its children and youth under an atheistic philosophy of education.

Rev. Kim Nam Soo, the Korean founder of Promise Ministries in New York City, began visiting North Korea in 1993 with the intention of traveling throughout the nation looking for ways to meet the needs of the people. Moved by his firsthand experience in that restrictive place, his highest priority became the training of children with the goal of instilling within them a biblical worldview and commitment to the Creator God. His experience was a transformational moment in his life that resulted in a strong personal commitment.

In North Korea, Rev. Kim Nam Soo observed the deep-seated effects

of raising a child with an atheistic mind-set. He saw what happens when children are taken from their parents in early infancy and trained in a tightly controlled environment. It was clear that this educational tactic was designed to embed the agenda of the Communist state, and it has proven to be very effective in producing a hard-set foundation rarely shaken by influences such as persecution, famine, and changes within neighboring countries. Rev. Kim observed that soon after birth, a child is sent to a state-sponsored nursery and dedicated to the Communist regime and the "Great Leader." The child also learns about and celebrates the "Juche Idea" until fully accepting it as everything of importance in life.

"Juche," originally the North Korean version of Marxist Communism, has become a recognized world religion with more adherents than Judaism, Sikhism, Jainism, or Zoroastrianism. It has been studied, experimented with, and revised continually during the past 50 years. In North Korea it has become the "Dear Leader"-centric (Kim Jong II) religious nationalism, displacing and replacing all other religions. The North Korean child spends infancy and childhood in this environment, absorbing a prescribed view of creation, history, and the world. Without any choice, the child's life goals and life path are determined by outside forces.

Because of what he discovered in North Korea, Rev. Kim has reprioritized his global missions focus toward raising up children and youth from the 4/14 Window to know and serve God. A decade ago he began writing on the compelling need for a shift in missions strategies and resources toward this purpose. Although he is unable to intercede in the plight of children in North Korea, Rev. Kim is leading efforts on behalf of thousands of children in other nations, such as El Salvador and India. His example is inspiring others to do likewise for the 4/14 generation worldwide.

Physical/Health Challenge

One of the motivations for focusing on children is that they are suffering more than any other segment of society, often as a result of the sins of adults. Key statistics reveal the depth of this problem:

- More than 91 million children under five suffer from debilitating hunger.[37]
- Fifteen million children have been orphaned as a result of AIDS.[38]
- An estimated 265 million children have not been immunized against any diseases.[39]

Health interventions during childhood can prevent damage that is
virtually impossible to repair later in life. Addressing the physical and
emotional health issues of the young can result in significant advances
in lifelong well-being and personal development. Working to improve the
health of children not only provides them a more promising future, it
also creates an invaluable opportunity to minister to their families and

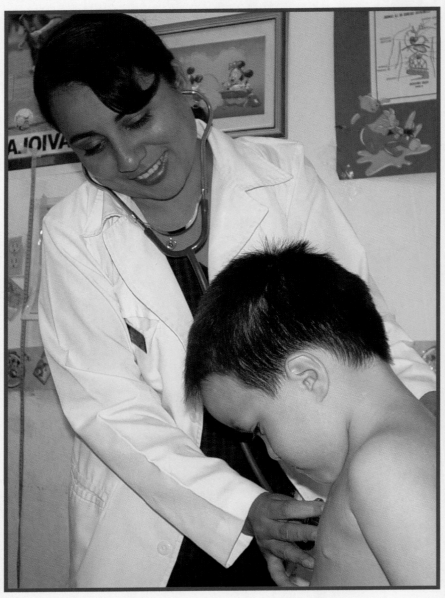

communities. In fact, strategic efforts to improve children's health can lead to the stability of entire nations.

Where do we begin to address this health problem? One of the principal approaches is through the establishment of a biblical worldview, which is holistic in nature and deals with the entire person. Jesus not only ministered to the soul; He healed physical disabilities and diseases as a central part of His ministry. He taught and equipped His disciples to do the same. From that point on, Jesus commissioned His church to be the ongoing working of Christ in the world, to bring healing and physical restoration wherever possible.

The Outcome of a Biblical Worldview: Transformation of a Nation's Health

There are many challenges to good health in the developing world today, such as clean water, proper sanitation, vaccination against childhood diseases, and so on, but none has received more attention than the AIDS pandemic. A new initiative in Swaziland aims to teach every child a biblical perspective on HIV and AIDS. As of this writing, more than 47,000 children have received this vital instruction—teaching that can literally save their lives. Each child is guided through an innovative program called I Matter, a series of 10 sessions aimed at instilling a healthy self-esteem, a sense of individual value, and a biblical understanding of life.[40]

The HIV/AIDS epidemic has been a well-publicized health crisis, and many of its victims have been innocent children. United Nations (UN) officials estimated that in 2007 about 33 million people worldwide are HIV-positive, most of them in sub-Saharan Africa.[41] For years, the news about this pandemic grew steadily worse, but now things are changing in some hard-hit areas. In fact, the full-scale reversal of AIDS is underway in the country where the crisis began—Uganda. Dr. Edward Green, a medical anthropologist at Harvard University, acknowledges that this turnaround is due primarily to a change in values.[42]

In 1983 AIDS in Uganda was commonly called "the slim disease" due to its physically wasting characteristics. By 1992 the life expectancy of Ugandans had dropped to 42 years, and by 1993 nearly one in three persons in Uganda's capital, Kampala, carried the AIDS virus. No country in the world needed social transformation more than this nation.

Yet in only a decade, significant transformation began to occur there. By 2004 only 6% of the population was reported to be HIV-positive, a

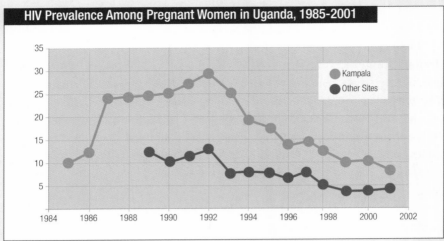

HIV Prevalence Among Pregnant Women in Uganda, 1985-2001

Data Source: Ministry of Health, Kampala

remarkable reduction from the cases recorded in 1993. The story of this dramatic reversal can be attributed to various people who recognized the crisis and were moved to respond. One of these individuals was Stephen Langa, a Ugandan businessman who now serves as the director of Family Life Network. Langa's approach was based upon a biblical worldview and a respect for, and obedience to, the Word of God.

Langa founded an non-governmental organization (NGO) in partnership with Uganda's first lady, Janet Museveni. Looking back to those critical days, she says, "This was more than a disease, it was a national disaster. Our only hope was to sound an alarm."[43] So, sound an alarm, they did, through the launching of a nationwide True Love Waits campaign that introduced abstinence education into the schools.

Schools would close down for four hours at a time to allow us to bring True Love Waits in to teach the students.[44] Based unapologetically on a biblical worldview, True Love Waits made an impact, changing attitudes and transforming behavior.

Langa says that behavioral change with a biblical worldview has three primary foundations:

1) The identity of a human being as a person made in the image of God.

2) The nature of the present reality, with an the appreciation of both the spiritual and physical world.

3) The future focus, with an understanding that history is going (biblically speaking) toward a glorious ending, in contrast to the

traditional African cultural perspective that defines life as an indefinite and often vicious cycle.

Langa articulated these positions with several other authors who drafted a policy on abstinence and faithfulness entitled *Uganda National Abstinence and Being Faithful Policy and Strategy on Prevention of Transmission of HIV.*[45]

On July 2, 2007, a debate raged in the U.S. House of Representatives over an amendment that would have reinstated funding for abstinence education programs to fight AIDS in Africa. Dr. Edward Green, one of the world's foremost experts on the HIV/AIDS pandemic, appeared as a witness at the hearings. Dr. Green stated that he was opposed to the Ugandan model at first, particularly with its emphasis on abstinence. However, he changed his opinion after he saw the success of the program in Uganda.[46]

Dr. Green's testimony before Congress affirmed the transformational impact of the Ugandan model comparable to other nations. This approach also brought positive social change to six other African nations in their battle against AIDS: Kenya, Zimbabwe, Ethiopia, Namibia, Tanzania, and Zambia.

Economic Challenge

The physical health needs of children and youth are closely related to the broader problems of poverty. The staggering reality is that more than one billion of the world's children—56%—are living in poverty or severe deprivation![47] A stunning 37% of the world's children—more than 674 million[48]—live in absolute poverty. Additionally, children living in what is defined as "severe deprivation" struggle with a "lack of income and productive resources to ensure sustainable livelihoods." They are also victims of "hunger and malnutrition, ill health, limited access or lack of access to education and other basic services, increased morbidity and mortality from illness, homelessness and inadequate housing, unsafe environments, social discrimination and exclusion."[49]

Raising up a new generation from the 4/14 Window to transform the world demands we address the physically poor among 4/14ers.

The map at the top of the next page indicates degrees of poverty in various shades of green. It also demonstrates higher youth populations through column heights. It is readily apparent that India, China, Nigeria, Democratic Republic of the Congo, and Ethiopia represent strategic

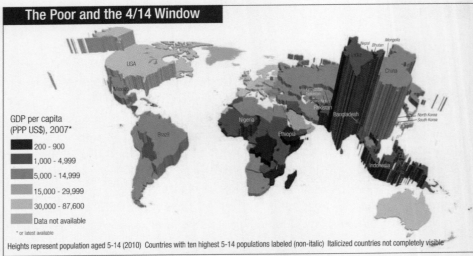

The Poor and the 4/14 Window

GDP per capita
(PPP US$), 2007*

- 200 - 900
- 1,000 - 4,999
- 5,000 - 14,999
- 15,000 - 29,999
- 30,000 - 87,600
- Data not available

* or latest available

Heights represent population aged 5-14 (2010)   Countries with ten highest 5-14 populations labeled (non-italic)   Italicized countries not completely visible

Sources: World Factbook; United Nations   Map by Global Mapping International, Jan. 2009

opportunities for focused transformational action among the poor in the 4/14 age group:

- Over one-third of children live in dwellings with more than five people per room.
- An estimated 134 million children have no access to any school whatsoever.
- More than half a billion children have no toilet facilities whatsoever.
- Almost half a billion children lack access to published information of any kind.
- An estimated 376 million children have more than a 15-minute walk to water and/or are using unsafe water sources.[50]

Of special concern amongst the poor in the 4/14 window are the millions of orphans. Indeed, God makes them His own special concern throughout Scripture, so His concern must be ours as well. The overwhelming lack of one-on-one holistic care for orphans makes them one of the most neglected groups in the 4/14 Window.

According to the World Health Organization, 85% of the world's orphans are between the ages of 4 and 14.[51] Orphaned girls are easy targets for sexual exploitation, due in part to a lowered self-image, loss of family structure, and psychological distress. Orphaned boys within the 4/14 Window often turn to crime or drugs and are prone to become abusive in adult relationships. This is largely the result of an absence of

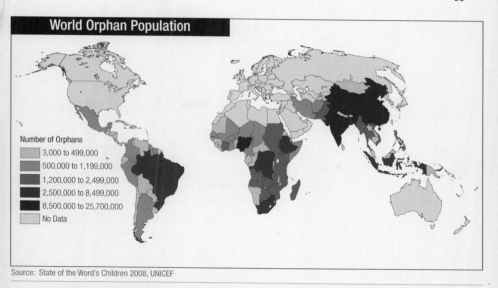

World Orphan Population

Number of Orphans

- 3,000 to 499,000
- 500,000 to 1,199,000
- 1,200,000 to 2,499,000
- 2,500,000 to 8,499,000
- 8,500,000 to 25,700,000
- No Data

Source: State of the Word's Children 2008, UNICEF

male leadership, mentorship, or protection. In many nations, boys are easy prey for evil men who bully them into forced labor or recruit them for participation in rebel armies (groups that find abandoned children to be easy fodder to fuel their separatist agendas). According to the Coalition to Stop the Use of Child Soldiers, at least 300,000 children, many as young as ten years old, are currently participating as child soldiers in armed conflicts around the world.

The Outcome of the Transformation of the Poverty of a Nation: God's People Equipped for Nation Building

The outcome of God's transforming power in a nation occurs as God's people are reconciled and raised up to fulfill His purposes in building a nation. For the term *transformation* to be properly applied to a community, change must be evident not only in the lives of its inhabitants but also in the fabric of its institutions. Its people must have sufficient health to work productively; they must have sufficient resources to meet basic needs and live above the level of deprivation and poverty. George Otis Jr., president of the Sentinel Group, a Christian research and information agency says, "A transformed community emerges when both the people and institutions have been overrun by the Kingdom of God."[52] The river of life begins to flow in the communities where death has reigned, and the result is the healing of the nation (Revelation 22).

The story of the transformation of Rwanda is one of reconciliation and instruction, with a particular emphasis on educating the nation's future leaders through a biblical worldview. The Rwandan genocide was fraught with senseless horror. Already among the poorest African countries, Rwanda harbored some of the worst communal and ethnic tensions in the world. During the heat of the genocide, the sound of a whistle would signal the start and end of the killing. Afterward, organizers would take a body count. The murderers used machetes, clubs, guns and any blunt instrument they could find to inflict as much pain on their victims as possible. No Tutsi was spared, and it wasn't enough to kill them; the intent was for them to suffer as severely as possible. As a direct result, more than 15% of the children in Rwanda are orphans of genocide; another 2% are HIV/AIDS orphans.

Between April and mid July of 1994, in a span of only 100 days, an estimated 800,000 to 900,000 Rwandans were slaughtered. Every minute of the day, someone, somewhere was being murdered, screaming for mercy but receiving none—10,000 every day, 400 every hour, 7 every minute.

Fearing Rwanda could lose an entire generation, Bishop John Rucyahana has founded orphanages and schools with a special focus on

those orphaned by the genocide and by AIDS. He says,

> One of the projects in which we have invested in a significant
> way is Sonrise School. We have over a thousand students to
> date, and more than half of the students are orphans. Some
> of them saw their parents hacked to death, but today are
> young men and women beaming with hope. Not that their
> past is forgotten, but it is forgiven. They know that they
> need to exchange the disparity for hope. We do prepare them
> for future servant leadership and challenge them to make
> a better nation of Rwanda. This is reflected, therefore, in
> the transformation of their character and their academic
> performance, but we don't forget that all of this springs from
> the fact that they know the source of their healing and the
> source of their transformation is love from the Lord Jesus
> Christ empowering us to love them and serve them.
>
> I am happy to share with you that this year (2009) all
> our students have passed the national exam, both in the
> elementary school and high school. One of our students was the
> second-best in the whole nation, and the first in mathematics
> and languages. The school is ranked among the top ten in the
> country. That's how good the school is academically. From the
> time we opened our doors at Sonrise, we have never had a
> student experience a post-traumatic panic attack. This does
> not mean that we have a supernatural school, but we seriously
> work hard in counseling our students and challenge them with
> the responsibility they have in the future for the nation. This
> makes them able not only to study but to know and conceive
> that they have a duty for themselves and for the nation. That
> processes their healing very quickly. We have also been able to
> protect them from the stigmatic experience, because we mix
> them with students who have families.[53]

The Challenge, Part 2: Maximizing Transformational Impact

Relational Challenge

Most of us are aware of these and other telling statistics about the needs of poor children around the world. But the fact is that it is not just poor children who are at risk. Actually, all children are at risk. Millions are at risk from poverty, but millions are also at risk from prosperity! Many children and young people today have everything to live with, but nothing to live for.[54] At the deepest level, poverty is what happens to people whose relationships do not work for their well-being. A person's well-being is rooted in wholesome relationships.

Oxford Statement on Children at Risk

The Oxford Statement on Children at Risk asserts God's passionate concern for needy children:

> Scripture clearly shows that God is outraged about what is happening to children. Over and over again God's warning throughout the Bible is "Don't touch my precious children!" (Exodus 22:22-24, Psalm 68:5, Ezekiel 16:4-14, Deuteronomy 24:17, etc.). God indicates terrible consequences for anyone harming His children: " . . . it would be better that a millstone be hung around his neck and [he] be drowned in the depths of the sea" (Matthew 18:6).

> As Christians then, we gladly acknowledge that our profound concern for children at risk flows from God Himself and our commitment to Jesus Christ. Most fundamentally, we affirm

that children, born and unborn, along with the rest of humanity, are created in the image of God and therefore have intrinsic worth (Genesis 1:27, Psalm 139:13-14). Any actions that demean, devalue or otherwise diminish children are sinful. Unfortunately, we live in a world where an attitude of cynicism towards the dignity of human life has resulted in a tragic loss of respect for humankind. Increasingly, children are the undeserving victims of human and demonic forces. The criminal waste of children's lives is an indictment upon all societies and cries out to God for vengeance.[55]

The Outcome of a Biblical Worldview: Transformation of Relationships Resulting in Shalom Communities

Transformation involves seeking positive changes in the whole of human life, materially, socially, and spiritually, by recovering our true identity as human beings created in the image of God and discovering our true

vocation as productive stewards, faithfully caring for our world and people.[56] This description of transformation addresses the core issues of identity and vocation.

Restoration of human relationships is rooted in our spiritual relationship with God. This results in *shalom* communities that are the visible fruit of a transformed world. A shalom community enjoys relational harmony, freedom, and justice for all. It allows everyone in the community to flourish while delighting in their relationship with God.

Shalom communities begin in the home, for at the heart of our earthly existence are family relationships. OneHope, an international children's evangelism ministry, has observed a dominant global trend of decaying family relationships, specifically associated with the problem of absentee fathers. There has never been a more glaring need for turning the hearts of the fathers toward their children.[57]

In South Asia, the problem is estrangement. In Russia, it is an issue of commitment when three-quarters of 1,500 secondary school girls surveyed said they would not stay with their husbands if they were not happy in their marriages. In Latin America, the issue is the abandonment of children by their fathers. A survey of 14,000 youth there showed a clear gap between beliefs about God and behaviors related to God. The influence of parents is high even though parents have invested smaller amounts of time in the lives of their children.

Interestingly, youth in Latin America and Spain express a desire to spend more time with their parents. Against popular opinion, many children actually wish for their parents to spend more time with them. In most of the countries surveyed, parents spend on average less than one hour a week with their children. Parents in much of the world have influence but invest little time. The world's children are calling out for the hearts of their fathers to be turned back to their sons and daughters.

One Person Can Make a Difference

A meeting took place in El Salvador recently with half a dozen former gang members incarcerated for serious crimes.[58] Each one told stories of absent, violent, neglectful fathers, most of them lured by promises of a better income in "the North" at a terrible cost to their wives and children. As children, these men found themselves duped into joining notorious gangs. Years of warfare in the 1970s and 1980s were followed by years of rampant crime, turning El Salvador into the most violent country in the world based upon the number of homicides per 1,000 people.

This was the deplorable condition in her nation when Martha Aurelia Martinez experienced a transforming moment—a moment that shifted her life focus to the 4/14 Window. Martha had a heart for children even as a teenager, and that compassion led her to become a medical doctor with a specialty in pediatrics. She began committing her time to national initiatives that would benefit thousands of Salvadoran children. That commitment continued to grow, prompting her to accept a call to serve on the international board of directors of World Vision International (WVI).

Meanwhile, she watched the condition of El Salvador's children become more and more desperate. In June 2004, at a gathering of the WVI international board in Bangkok, Martha had a dream of giving herself full time in ministry to El Salvador's children. On her knees, in tears, she answered God's call, dedicating her life to raising up the girls and boys of her country to become agents of change for future generations.

Dr. Martinez now serves as World Vision's director for El Salvador. She is living out the dream that God put in her heart that summer of 2004. During a recent Transform Latin America Summit, Martha facilitated the track for children and youth with the vision of seeking their transformation in conformity with the principles and values of God throughout Latin America. The world is sitting in darkness waiting for the revelation of the sons and daughters of God, who alone can turn "the heart of the fathers to the children and the children to the fathers" (Malachi 4:6). Dr. Martinez is one whose heart was turned to raise up the next generation, and she encourages us to do the same.

Social Challenge

Children and young adolescents have much to contribute to positive social change. What often prevents this from occurring is an absence of adults who believe in them. As a consequence, many 4/14ers do not believe in themselves. Nevertheless, most children and young people respond well to challenges and can participate in opportunities to better their surroundings and their societies.

It is unfortunate that today's 4/14ers are too often sheltered from such challenges and not given opportunities to use and develop their gifts. Many adults have a mistaken idea that children are stressed out and so should not be "burdened" with additional responsibilities. But, as William Damon, author of the book *Greater Expectations,* reminds us, "Contrary to what some adults think, they really do not need to come home after their six-hour day and 'cool out' in front of the TV. They do need to have their energies fully and joyfully engaged in worthwhile pursuits. Stress for a child is not a function of keeping busy; rather, it is a function of receiving conflicting messages about the self and experiencing troublesome life events beyond one's control. Activities that children gain satisfaction from, and accomplishments that children are proud of, relieve rather than induce stress. Activities that provide genuine services to others are ideal in this regard."[59]

The fact is that where children and young people are given a significant challenge—intentionally by wise adults or "accidentally" through necessity or disaster or obligation—they usually readily adapt to such demands. Given such challenges, Damon notes that children have always "pitched in with energy and pride, with all the natural vigor of childhood. Such experiences gave these children invaluable opportunities to learn personal and social responsibility. In an old-fashioned phrase, they were character-building experiences."[60]

William Damon continues:

> By systematically underestimating the child's capabilities, we are limiting the child's potential for growth. In withholding from children the expectation to serve others . . . we are preventing them from acquiring a sense of social and personal responsibility. We are leaving the child to dwell on nothing more noble than gratifying the self's moment-by-moment inclinations. In the end, this orientation is a particularly unsatisfying form of self-centeredness, because it creates a focus on a personal self that has no special skills or valued services to offer anyone else. Paradoxically, by giving the child purposes that go beyond the self, an orientation to service results in a more secure belief in oneself.[61]

The Outcome of God's Supernatural Power in Response to the Social Challenge: Freedom and Uplift for People

In 2005, according to United Nations records, Norway ranked as the number one nation in the world in terms of human development.[62] The UN concept of human development incorporates several elements: wealth, life expectancy, education, human freedom, dignity, and human agency (the role of people in development). It is notable that Norway is ranked as the second country in the world in per-capita giving. Norway has emerged in each of the first six years of the 21st century as a model of a developed human community. What is the explanation for this?

In a *Dagbladet* article published on June 11, 1998, Arild Stubhaug, an expert on the formation of Norway, attributed the success of contemporary Norway to a young man who was the simple son of a farmer.[63] Stubhaug wrote the account of Hans Nielsen Hauges' encounter with God on April 5, 1796. His life and work led to democratic movements among both the farmers and the people living in the cities and towns.

Transformational Communities

Another demonstration of how God has worked in an urban setting through His body is found in the work of a single church in São Paulo, Brazil, that brought new life to one of the most dangerous and impoverished parts of the city. The east side has slowly been elevated from lower to middle class because of the ministry of one local church pastored by Carlos Becerra. *Comunidade da Graça* (Community of Grace) has adopted 900 at-risk families.

In the 1990s, a former, decaying public school in the area was overrun by 150 homeless families. The place became a distribution point for drugs. Armed thugs guarded the doors. Yet only a few blocks away, a Christian community urgently interceded for these people. In addition to

their prayers, they began visiting the families and demonstrating the love of Christ in practical ways.

Ten years later, the area that had suffered abject poverty, poor housing, crime, and floods has witnessed a dramatic transformation. In 2002, with the help of the church, the homeless families were referred to municipal housing programs, and 360 children are being cared for and prepared to go on God's mission of transformation. All this took place in the same building that had once been a haven for drugs and a refuge for the homeless. Today a foundation established by the church is one of the main non-governmental organizations in Brazil serving the poor and seeking to raise them up through social development, improved health, and the practice of holistic mission.

"Untouchables"

A third example of transformation comes from the contemporary struggle for freedom for India's hundreds of millions of "untouchables." It reveals how God is working through His people to bring about a reformation that may prove to be akin to the Protestant Reformation.

The challenge of raising up the 4/14ers in places of persecution is an important and difficult one. The restrictive systems and structures that strangle religious freedom and govern the spread of the gospel in these nations makes access to their children a complicated and sometimes dangerous prospect. Yet this is a challenge worth accepting.

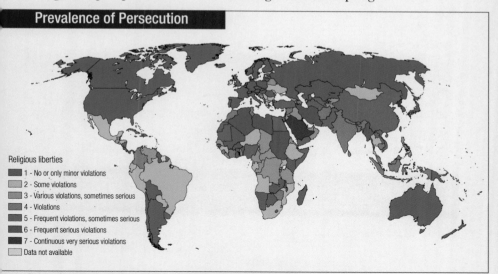

Prevalence of Persecution

Religious liberties
1 - No or only minor violations
2 - Some violations
3 - Various violations, sometimes serious
4 - Violations
5 - Frequent violations, sometimes serious
6 - Frequent serious violations
7 - Continuous very serious violations
Data not available

ource: Christian Solidarity International   Map by Global Mapping International, Jan. 2009

The map on the previous page demonstrates where violations of freedom create uniquely difficult conditions. This is most apparent in the incidences related to the Dalit people of India. The Dalits are history's longest-standing oppressed people, and today they constitute the largest number of people who are victims of slavery. According to Joseph D'Souza, more than 250 million Dalits are denied their basic human rights and dignity.[64] For thousands of years they have been directly and indirectly oppressed, often quite cruelly.

India's caste system is rooted in an ancient myth that the four major castes were birthed out of the body of God. The lowest caste was said to come out of the feet of God. Yet because the Dalits were not believed to have come from the body of God at all, they were, and still are, considered outcasts and untouchables; and, according to the myth, they are to be treated as if they were never born. As a result, Dalits endure painful shame and rejection and a sense of hopelessness that is so culturally ingrained in them, only the transformative work of the Lord Jesus can remake their worldview. The word *dalit* actually means "broken" or "crushed." The Dalits represent 250 million (24%) of India's total population.[65]

God's transformational acts in history have always included freedom from oppression, a concern for human rights and justice, and a clear stand against all forms of racism. From the time of the Exodus of the people of Israel to the time of William Wilberforce's struggle against the slave trade to the present day, God continues to call His people to engage in transformational work in the arenas of justice, mercy, and reconciliation.

The Scriptures tell us that when God created people, He did so after His own likeness: "So God created man in his own image, in the image of God he created him; male and female he created them" (Genesis 1:27). There are no distinctions or rankings of gender or caste in humankind's creation. There are no "outcastes" in God's original design. No one should be treated as though he or she were never born.

After 25 years as a missionary, Joseph D'Souza describes the transformative moment that caused him to turn his attention to the Dalit children. He saw the answer through education focusing on the development of a biblical worldview and a mastery of the English language. Says D'Souza:

> It was in the year 2000 that we ended up in a major meeting with the Dalit leadership. They encouraged us to do Jesus'

mission among them and not to be on the defensive in the
light of the attacks on the Christians by the extremist Hindu
forces. The two Dalit leaders were Udit Raj[66] and Professor
Kancha Ilaiah.[67]

When I asked them what mission of Jesus would they like
us to do among the Dalits, they said, "Free our children.
Free them by giving them quality English-medium school
education with a biblical worldview that teaches about the
equality of human beings, their value as humans, and the fact
that Jesus loves them."

When probed further they asked whether we were aware that
there were more than 40 million child laborers in India, whether
we knew that of the 15 million children who were in some form
of bondage the vast majority were either scheduled caste or
scheduled tribe children, whether we were aware again that the

vast number of children trafficked in the sex trade were again from the Dalit and "backward caste" backgrounds.

Finally they pointed out that to break the cycle of slavery among the Dalits, we had to break it before the children began to think of themselves as slaves, as untouchables, as criminal tribes, as forsaken and punished by God in this life and as being worthless.

I was already in mission work for 25 years when this encounter happened in my life and in the organizations I lead. I clearly saw that the key to Dalit transformation, the key to transformation of India, and the key to kingdom impact in India was to free Dalit and other low-caste children.

Thus by 2010 we will have the first 100 schools. This has resulted in my involvement in the justice issue for the Dalit people. The Dalit leaders in the nation of India believe us because we responded to their cry for freedom, which began in their cry for the freedom of their children.

Thus the vision of 1,000 schools was born—seeking to provide access to education for every Dalit. The English language would allow them access to all jobs, not just the most menial jobs. The biblical worldview would help all Dalits to discover their true identity as children of God made in His own image. It would enhance the likelihood that religious freedom would be practiced in every place throughout India.[68]

Ministry Challenge

The ministry challenge is about encouraging and equipping the children and youth of the 4/14 Window to use their gifts and potential as agents in transforming the world. They represent an enormous untapped pool of influencers with sensitivity to the voice of God and willingness to do His bidding. I need to reemphasize that God can and does use children and young people—their prayers, their insights, their hands, and their feet—in changing the hearts of humankind.

The 4/14ers have great capacity to understand the faith, and great courage and effectiveness as they share it. Adults will fail the 4/14ers if we fail to equip them with the vision and opportunity to do something beyond themselves. Indeed, many churches discourage children and young people from finding and developing their natural gifts and aptitudes for character and competence in areas like missions awareness.

Much of what passes for children's ministry in churches today is geared to entertaining rather than equipping or challenging them. It is okay for children and youth to have fun, but there are missed opportunities in making that the focus. We must ask, what are our children *not* doing and *not* learning while they are being entertained?

Alex and Brett Harris were 18 years old when they wrote a book called *Do Hard Things*. The Harris boys note, that "being considered a good teen only requires that we don't do bad stuff like taking drugs, drinking, and partying. But is it enough to know of the negative things we don't do?"[69]

The 4/14ers thrive on challenges. They love opportunities to gain skills and to prove themselves. Generally they respond with energy and enthusiasm when provided opportunities to test their abilities. When denied such challenges, they can become insecure and apathetic.[70] And could there be a more exciting and life-changing challenge than learning about the world, sharing God's love for its peoples, and transforming a generation?

Let us not forget that 4/14ers are capable of engaging in spiritual warfare. They have great capacity for fighting spiritual battles through their childlike faith. God is no respecter of persons! He can anoint children with the Holy Spirit just as He empowered the apostle Paul and the disciples. Children are sensitive to the Holy Spirit's leading because they have not yet developed the spiritual barriers that many adults have erected over the course of their lives.

The Outcome of Ministering Children: Increased Faith in God, Answered Prayer, and Shalom Communities

One illustration of how God is using children as agents of transformation today comes from one of the most conflict-ridden areas in the world, representing one of the most challenging cultural clashes of our time.

From 1998 to 2006, the central Sulawesi region of Indonesia was torn by violence between Muslim and Christian communities. Terrorism, bombings, beheadings, and rapes plagued the villages of Sulawesi. Hundreds died and thousands more were forced from their homes. In the

year 2000 alone, 500 homes were burned. Today, that state of chaos is changing because of a spiritual revival. An eyewitness reported, "People are hearing a message of reconciliation from an unusual source: an eight-year-old boy. Because of this, the villages in that area once being consumed by bloodshed are now being transformed."

Today, Muslim residents of the city of Poso, who were previously unable to cross into Kawua, are able to do so. Christians can also interact with their Muslim neighbors. The central market, formerly a Muslim stronghold, is now a place where members of the two previously warring communities shop together.

"The miracle is so real and right in front of us. Why is it that we don't believe it?" Adlan Moko Molewe, . . . boy preacher, said as the crowd intently listened to him. While the crowds worship, Moko's eight-year-old friend, Selfin, prays for a touch from God. When interviewed by CBN News, Moko, who is himself a refugee whose family home was destroyed, said, "I think the Lord wants us to have peace in Poso. . . . The Lord wants us to have one heart. We should love one another."[71]

When Pastor Rinaldy Daminik of the Sulawesi Christian Church was interviewed about what is happening, he answered, "I believe the Lord is using the children to call for repentance and great transformation in Poso. We can say this is the seed of the martyrs' blood in Poso. Their blood poured out in this land is now bearing fruit through Moko and Selfin."[72] The result is a more peaceful province.

Baharuddin, a Muslim who experienced miraculous healing, said, "I like it when everybody with different beliefs is praising God. I saw how the Christian people treat us nicely, even if we are Muslim. I told my friend: You see it is possible that Christians and Muslims live harmoniously."[73]

Yus Mangun, a Poso community figure who is now a member of the Central Sulawesi Legislative Council, reported that communal riots, which escalated into sectarian conflict, no longer exist. Gone are the days when people, concentrated in large mobs, attacked and burned down villages.[74]

All of this is through the work of an eight-year-old preacher. Yes, some adults don't get it. They think children could not be ministering in this way and with this kind of impact. Others have stopped to consider the spiritual life and capacity to minister that is within a child. One of these is Robert Coles, who writes about it in *The Spiritual Life of Children*. He provides overwhelming anecdotal

evidence that children connect with God on many levels.[75] Coles notes
that the discovery of what may lie within a child's spiritual being is
rewarding for the adult who listens carefully. The way a child talks
about God and the world has an innocence and purity to it that is often
lost by adults in this age of multitasking.

The potential for children engaged in the ministry of prayer cannot
be underestimated. John Robb, chairman of the International Prayer
Council and the Children's Prayer Network, believes that some of the
praying children of today will become rulers of nations tomorrow. Many
more will be influential for Christ in their generation, bringing His
transformation to our world. There is a window of spiritual receptivity in
children between the ages of 4 and 14. Like the prophet Samuel, they have
a greater openness to hearing God's voice, and this is the time to nurture
them and invest in their futures. After age 14, it can be much harder for
them to give their lives to Christ.

In 2002, John Robb experienced a transforming moment that led to
his prioritizing the role of children in prayer ministry. He was reading
Luke 10:17-21 and realized that Jesus was teaching that the spiritual
authority He was offering to tread on serpents and scorpions was
revealed to little children.

"It was that year that I decided with a couple of colleagues to
begin assessing the impact of children's prayers on transformational
development efforts."[76] Robb was amazed by the results in the seven
countries that were part of the pilot project. The Children in Prayer (CiP)
movement began to spread within the organization until about 20 offices
got involved. He eventually devoted his full efforts to this international
prayer movement.

Research across different locations where prayer programs were
led by children demonstrates astonishing results of transformation and
answered prayers, such as

- relatives being healed from sickness
- community splits being healed
- parents and community leaders coming to faith in Christ
- clean water and clinics becoming available, even with the
  government choosing at the very time of prayer to provide a well
  or clinic in their specific locations
- students achieving better grades and performing at higher
  academic levels

It is the clear testimony of Scripture that God has chosen to work in human history through the intercessory prayers of His people—including children. In fact, children may be the most powerful source of prayer for community and national transformation.

Psalm 8:2 says that there is power in the prayers and praises of children: "You have established a stronghold from the mouths of children . . . to silence the enemy and the avenger" (HCSB).

Robb comments, "Our work with children is all about introducing them to a life of intimacy with the Lord through prayer. Prayer is the way we relate directly to God, so this work is fulfilling Jesus' command to enable children to come into relationship with Him, a relationship that will change their lives and transform the world around them."[77]

Jesus loved to have children around Him. Roy Zuck notes that "while few of the world's religious leaders have had regard for children, Jesus was different. Not only did He welcome them; He even used them to teach adults some essential spiritual lessons!"[78]

It was not just the Pharisees and the vendors in the temple who angered Jesus, but His own disciples did so on occasion. Once Jesus became "indignant" when they considered children too unimportant to warrant His attention (Mark 10:14). Might He also be indignant with those who are negligent and indifferent to the world's children today?

Holistic Approach to
Transformational Development

Transformational development is a process by which people become whole. It is characterized by growth, change, and learning. It is a process of becoming. The direction of development is always toward completeness. As Dan Brewster of Compassion International notes,

> It is not enough to improve only one dimension of a person's life and leave other dimensions in inadequacy. To treat parasitic infection is noble. But if a treated child is left in an unsanitary environment with contaminated water, the intervention is incomplete. If a child receives an education, but social structures prevent him from getting a job, the intervention is incomplete. If a person is introduced to faith in Christ and enjoys spiritual freedom but is left in poverty and oppression, the intervention is incomplete. The scope of development is toward completeness.[79]

Luke 2:52 provides a model for the kind of development involved in the 4/14 vision: "Jesus increased in wisdom and in stature and in favor with God and man." The verse cites four pivotal components: wisdom, stature, favor with God, and favor with man. It neatly encompasses all aspects of the whole person and provides a useful model for creating meaningful programs that produce holistic development. The objective of holistic Christian development is for every child to have the opportunity to grow and develop in each of these four areas.

Compassion International's holistic child-development program recognizes four integrated dimensions of child development that parallel Luke 2:52: physical (health), socioemotional (identity and social relationships), cognitive (education and skill development), and spiritual. Compassion's long-term commitment to individual child development

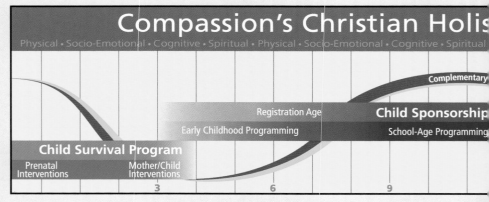

Compassion's Christian Holis...

Physical • Socio-Emotional • Cognitive • Spiritual • Physical • Socio-Emotional • Cognitive • Spiritual

Complementary

Registration Age

Child Sponsorship

Early Childhood Programming

School-Age Programming

Child Survival Program

Prenatal Interventions

Mother/Child Interventions

3   6   9

drives toward programmatic outcomes for children in each of those four areas of Christian holistic child development:

1) Demonstrates commitment to the lordship of Christ.
2) Chooses good health practices and is physically healthy.
3) Exhibits the motivation and skills to be economically self-supporting.
4) Interacts with other people in a healthy and compassionate manner.

Compassion believes that "releasing children from poverty in Jesus' name" (the organization's tagline) requires starting early and finishing well with a comprehensive program (see Compassion's Child Development Model). Compassion's program design and curriculum focus on individual children in order to raise a generation of servant catalysts who are agents of transformational development in their families, communities, and nations.

Compassion's development philosophy sees the child at the center of long-term transformation. The child is not, in the ultimate sense, an object of intervention but is ultimately an agent of intervention. Compassion maintains that a changed context can sometimes change people, but changed people, and changed children in particular, will ultimately change their context.

tic Child Development Model

Physical • Socio-Emotional • Cognitive • Spiritual • Physical • Socio-Emotional • Cognitive • Spiritual

Interventions

Leadership Development Program
Scholarship and Leadership Training

Program

Completion Age

Adolescent Programming

12   15   18   21

What is the Poverty Wheel?

Poverty is a complex problem. The poverty wheel is a graphic representation of the problem of poverty. The hub represents absolute poverty. The spokes represent the different needs of those in poverty. The rim represents enough. Compassion's mission is to bring children from the hub of the wheel (poverty) to the rim (enough).

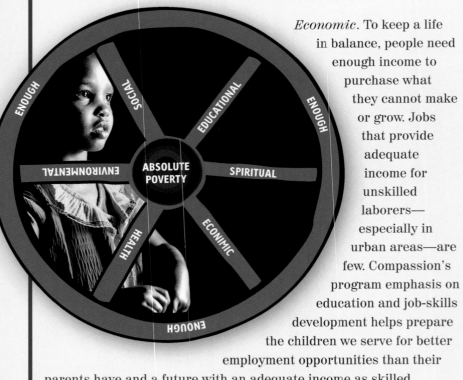

Economic. To keep a life in balance, people need enough income to purchase what they cannot make or grow. Jobs that provide adequate income for unskilled laborers—especially in urban areas—are few. Compassion's program emphasis on education and job-skills development helps prepare the children we serve for better employment opportunities than their parents have and a future with an adequate income as skilled, working adults.

Health. Physical and emotional health are the basis for our abilities to work, play and develop sound relationships. In many impoverished families, good health is no guarantee. That's why Compassion teaches children how to monitor their own health for common diseases and provides hygiene training. Compassion also offers medical interventions when more serious needs arise.

Environmental. Physical surroundings—climate, water supply, housing and land—all affect a person's well-being. The circumstances of poverty put children at particular environmental risk. Compassion's program helps children deal with their challenging environment and dream about how they can make it better for the future.

Social. A culture or government that devalues people—especially children—is an obstacle to releasing them from poverty. Children are the most vulnerable to being exploited as cheap labor, child soldiers or possessions. Compassion works within government and cultural systems to encourage the idea that children are a valuable resource. As such, children should be cherished—and given every opportunity to flourish.

Educational. New information combined with practical training is necessary to develop and maintain a life of adequacy. Children are often the best communicators of new information to their families. They are ready to adopt new ideas and adapt those ideas to work even better in their own communities. Compassion is committed to taking the best and most relevant information to the children we serve, so they can be effective change agents right where they live.

Spiritual. Without an understanding of the Word and ways of God, it is difficult to understand yourself. Nearly four-fifths of our world's children are growing up with no knowledge of God's love for them through Jesus Christ. Compassion works in many communities where Christianity is not the religion of the majority. We cannot—and will not—coerce any child or parent to become a Christian. But many have decided to follow Jesus as they experience God's love through the ministry of the local church partnering with Compassion. Children's lives undergo a revolution when they realize that God loves and values them. They understand that they were placed on the earth with a divine purpose in mind. Many go on to develop a deep commitment to discover and fulfill that purpose for God's glory.

(From Wess Stafford, *Too Small to Ignore,* [Colorado Springs: WaterBrook, 2005].)

World Vision's Blueprint

Another example of a holistic approach is that of World Vision International, as described by Jaisankar Sarma, International Director of Transformation Development.[80] The ministry focus is on bringing justice to the poor and needy, and of the poor and needy, none are more desperate and deserving than children.

World Vision International has prioritized transformational impact in order to affect the whole child, producing well-being in each developmental area. For instance, a child might grow in stature, but if the child doesn't grow in wisdom, he or she will be incapable of living a productive and meaningful life. A child who grows in wisdom, stature, and favor with people will be spiritually bankrupt if not led to favor with God. Holism is the process by which one experiences the "fullness of life" Jesus promised in John 10:10.

Sarma's definition of *transformational development* involves a process through which children, families, and communities move toward wholeness of life that brings dignity, justice, peace, and hope.[81] The broad scope of transformational development includes economic, political, environmental, social, and spiritual aspects of life at the local, national, and global levels.

Elements of Justice for the Poor and Needy

Impact on Children	• Child Immunization • Child Nutrition • Primary Education • Diarrhea Management
Community Well-Being	• Household Resilience • Poorest Households • Access to Safe Water • HIV/AIDS Prevention
Restoring Relationships	• Caring for Others • Emergence of Hope • Christian Impact
Community Ownership	• Community Participation • Social Sustainability
Transforming Systems	• Local Promotion of Justice

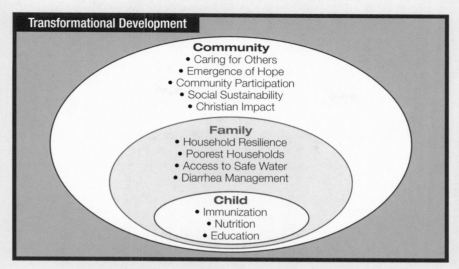

Human transformation, according to Sarma, is a continuous process of profound and holistic change brought about, ultimately, by the work of God. The process and the impact of transformational development are never divorced from the principles and values of the kingdom of God. Transformational development focuses on the following:

- the well-being of children, families, and communities
- the empowerment of all children as agents of transformation themselves
- the restoration of relationships
- communities that are interdependent and empowered
- transformed social systems that will empower another generation to begin within the transformed culture

In the second domain of change, girls and boys participate in the development process in an age-appropriate manner. This prepares them to be agents of transformation in their families and communities in the present and the future.

These community-based transformational indicators serve as key measures derived from the framework illustrated in the chart above. They provide a quantifiable basis for assessing the impact of transformational development programs and reveal whether these programs and processes are meeting their intended goals.

ConneXions Model for Leadership Development

Within the greater holistic approach, a particular emphasis is needed toward spiritual transformation and the development of healthy leaders from an early age. The ConneXions model of leader development outlined in the following sections provides a Christ-centered set of working principles.[82] It is a framework for life transformation that is widely applicable to the spiritual aspect of the transformation required to reach 4/14ers.

5Cs of Nurture

Our goal should be nothing less than the entire transformation of the lives of children as they are nurtured in five areas: Christ, community, character, calling, and competencies. Children first come to know God (Christ) by faith and become united with Him as the foundation of life

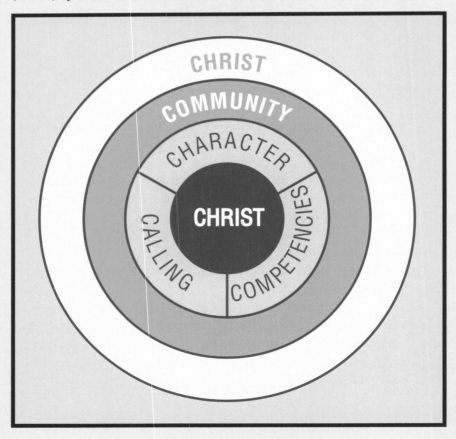

transformation. Their union with Christ is encouraged and strengthened through living and growing in a supportive and accountable family, surrogate family, and/or church (community). Within the context of community they grow in integrity (character), and are prepared to discover God's purpose for their lives (calling). Finally, they are nurtured in biblical knowledge, overall education, and life skills so that they might fulfill their calling with excellence (competencies). All of this needs to happen for 4/14ers in an effective, holistic, and transformational context.

Four Dynamics of the Transformational Process

As we pursue a holistic goal for the transformation of 4/14ers, we need holistic processes based on the clear example of Jesus. These transformational processes provide a sturdy framework and a guiding paradigm for the design of specific programs to transform the lives of children and youth in the 4/14 Window.

Look at how Jesus transformed His disciples, and you will discover a paradigm for raising up people who can change the world. His method can inform and guide our calling from God to transform the 4/14 Window.

In Mark 3:14-15, we see how Christ trained His disciples to become leaders: "He appointed twelve (whom he also named apostles) so that they might be with Him and He might send them out to preach and have authority

to cast out demons." This simple but profound statement distills how Jesus
built leaders. In short, He created a context that included four dynamics of
transformation: spiritual, relational, experiential, and instructional:

- a *spiritual* environment conducive to growth in relationship
  with Jesus and the Father through prayer
- a *relational* web including a mature mentor (Jesus) and other
  like-minded followers (the community of disciples)
- an *experiential* context involving challenging and diverse

SPIRITUAL

Children can fellowship with God and
enjoy Him.

Prayer for and with children is
essential.

Children are impacted by all the
spiritual disciplines.

Children can reflect on their own
lives.

EXPERIENTIAL

Families should teach their children
through example, nurture, and
correction.

Nurturing children takes place
spontaneously and naturally in the
course of life.

God has wired children to respond
positively to encouragement,
affirmation, and fun.

RELATIONAL

Parents have the primary responsibility for the spiritual growth of their
children.

Men should be the primary spiritual
leaders of the family.

Relational abilities are developed in
the home.

Healthy families are built and
sustained in the church community.

INSTRUCTIONAL

The Word of God is the basis for
growing godly children; it has the
power to transform their lives.

Parents and families have the
responsibility to teach their children.

Teaching children can occur at
predefined times, as well as spontaneously and naturally in daily life.

assignments that forced His followers to have cohesion between
their "action" and their "confession"

- an *instructional* dialogue where He taught them to see life
  from a new perspective—the kingdom of God

This transformational context produced nothing less than a total change of the disciples' lives and circumstances! The same careful approach can serve as an incubator for nurturing a generation of changed 4/14ers. The process would include:

Not only will this approach equip children to live meaningful lives, it will also help them

- find fulfillment in their relationship with God;
- garner the necessary knowledge and skills to impact their world; and
- gain a life purpose and mission.

These principles serve as a framework for transforming 4/14ers that can be applied in any context or culture. And while it does have structure, it is important to remember that this is a guiding paradigm, not a rigid program.

The four transformational dynamics can be applied to the design of family ministry programs, formal schools, Bible schools and seminaries, nonformal training programs, and mentoring/discipleship/lifestyle leadership programs, or any program aimed at bettering the lives of children.

When the four transformational dynamics are strongly present, children grow in the 5Cs:

- Christ: Spiritual life is nurtured.
- Community: Relational capacities are strengthened.
- Character is developed.
- Calling is clarified.
- Competencies: Leadership capacities are built.

This is how lives are changed; this is how leaders in the next generation will be raised up!

Transformational Environment

According to the Bible, the most appropriate transformational environment for children is the family. Parents have the primary responsibility for nurturing their offspring. The church's role is to encourage and equip them to do so.

Certainly, this is the "perfect world" scenario, and sadly, many 4/14ers do not have the privilege of being in a family setting or of having parents who are Christ followers—or having parents at all. But we can and should apply God's commands to parents in whatever "non-perfect-world" contexts we find ourselves with respect to reaching the 4/14 Window. God's guidance for parents can apply to caregivers, extended family, the local church, and ministry workers in situations where parents are absent or families are dysfunctional.

Through proper training in a family, children come to know Christ. Inward character and outward behaviors are formed; life skills and relational abilities are developed; and principles of mercy, righteousness, holiness, and love are learned (Ephesians 6:4). This truth has been lost in our time, and we need to return the child-training role to the family. This is a key paradigm shift.

The family is the very best place to grow in Christ. But in order for children to mature spiritually, parents or caregivers must take seriously their own responsibility to grow in Christ as role models for their children.

Biblical Pattern

We can see this in the example of Timothy (2 Timothy 3:10-17). His spiritual life was formed at home, in the church, and in his ministry, and in his personal relationship with Paul in a transformational collage of all four dynamics: spiritual, relational, experiential, and instructional.

God has called parents, extended family, caregivers, the local church, and ministry workers to present Him to the children in their care. They can do this in many ways:

- teaching them the Word of God
- sharing times of family worship, which can include singing, Bible study, prayer, and other spiritual activities
- seeking God together during special times as well as fellowshipping with Him in the normal course of daily life

Parents and caregivers present God to children by leading them through the experiences of life. It is the adult's responsibility to interpret the world to their children so that they will learn how to perceive and correctly understand the presence of God in all that happens. Adults also foster spiritual maturity in children by giving them age-appropriate responsibilities that build faith and develop practical life skills.

Living Example

Mya was 14 years old and about to graduate from middle school. She attended church but did not have a passion for God. Over a period of several months, she felt God's calling, sought the approval of her parents, and entered a local training school run by her church—a community with a holistic model of healthy leader development.

At first Mya found it quite different from what she expected, with challenging assignments, true relationship building, practical daily responsibilities, ministry opportunities, and challenges that deepened her spiritual growth. She didn't understand why the school was like this, but she found herself growing and changing. She was being transformed by the power of the Holy Spirit and the special assignments designed by her leaders that incorporated spiritual, relational, experiential, and teaching dynamics.

Soon after Mya graduated, she was given a stretching cross-cultural assignment that put her in difficult circumstances, ministering to children not much younger than herself in a remote region of the country. She had been well trained through holistic transformational experiences, and her ministry bore fruit. Because of the changes in these children's lives, many of their parents began searching for a meaningful relationship with Christ.

Myra returned home four years later and has continued to develop her leadership capabilities in her home church. At 22, she is a leader in their holistic learning community. She designs and facilitates learning experiences for students that build their spiritual lives, relationships, character, calling, and ministry skills. As a young girl, Mya was transformed through holistic training, and she is now actively involved in transforming the lives of others.

Conclusion

The ConneXions model introduces a new holistic paradigm into our efforts to transform the lives of children in the 4/14 Window. The 5Cs and the four dynamics are tools with which we can design and develop transformational programs. Parents, families, churches, schools, seminaries, child advocates, relief ministries, and others can implement these principles in culturally appropriate and contextually sensitive ways that foster holistic transformation in the 4/14 Window.

Epilogue

Raising Up a New Generation to Transform Our World

I began this book with a call for a new missional focus: Just as the 10/40 Window focused our attention on "the core of the core," so the 4/14 Window is meant to focus our attention on the "central core of the core." My purpose has been to turn the spotlight on children and youth in the 4/14 Window—the decade of opportunity. We have seen that this is an enormous people group—one that is suffering neglect and exploitation. At the same time, these precious 4/14ers are also the most receptive people group on the planet.

Both their receptivity as subjects for holistic mission and their untapped potential as agents for transformational mission have been

largely overlooked by the church. That's one reason I wrote this book. It is an urgent appeal to consider the potential and the strategic importance of the 1.2 billion children and youth in the 4/14 Window. It is also a plea to open our hearts and minds to the challenge of raising up a new generation that can be transformed and mobilized as agents to change the world.

In these pages I have presented the tremendous needs and timely opportunities to reach 4/14ers in every nation. I have outlined the importance of a holistic ministry approach to these children, and I have called the body of Christ to give priority to training and mobilizing them to carry out the church's mission.

I close with another invitation: to join with many others around the globe who are waking up and reaching out to this remarkable group. They are reading Scripture again with the "child in the midst" (Mark 9:36) and are realizing that 4/14ers are present everywhere throughout the Bible— very often in transformational roles. They are seeing that we are to care for and nurture children because they are so close to the heart of God. They are concluding that we must take the 4/14ers seriously, because God surely does!

Realizing the need to reprioritize my own missional focus on the 4/14 Window was a transforming moment for me, as it was for those in the case studies I have cited. James Loder, in his book *The Transforming Moment,* says, "Moments of transforming significance radically reopen the question of reality."[83] I pray that reading this book will cause you to experience your own transforming moment—an awakening to the need for change and saying yes to intentional engagement in raising up a new generation from the 4/14 Window to change the world.

About Compassion International

Compassion International is a Christian holistic child-development ministry working to release over one million children from poverty. More than 50 years of child-development experience have shaped Compassion's understanding of children and childhood as critically important for individual, family, community, and national transformation. Through sponsorship, Compassion connects an individual sponsor with a child to protect and develop that child while simultaneously equipping the sponsor as an informed child advocate. All child-development programs are implemented in partnership with local Christian churches.

The Compassion Difference

Christ-centered: Everything Compassion is and does points to the lordship of Jesus Christ.

Child-focused: Compassion commits to the long-term individual development of each child.

Church-partnered: Compassion partners with more than 5,000 indigenous churches to equip them for child ministry because the church is the hope of the world.

Compassion's Mission Statement

Releasing children from poverty in Jesus' name

In response to the Great Commission, Compassion International exists as an advocate for children, to release them from their spiritual, economic, social, and physical poverty and enable them to become responsible and fulfilled Christian adults.

To learn more, visit www.compassion.com.

Endnotes

1. Luis Bush, *The 10/40 Window: Getting to the Core of the Core* (Colorado Springs, CO: AD2000 & Beyond) http://www.ad2000.org/1040broc.htm (accessed February 17, 2009).

2. Wikipedia, s.v. "10/40 Window," http://en.wikipedia.org/wiki/10/40_Window (accessed May 5, 2009). (I invite you to read my rationale about this area's strategic importance at http://www.ad2000.org/1040broc.htm and weigh the facts for yourself.)

3. Bryant Myers, "The State of the World's Children: A Cultural Challenge to the Christian Mission in the 1990s" (presentation delivered at an Evangelical Foreign Mission Association executive retreat).

4. National Intelligence Council, *Global Trends 2025: A World Transformed* (November 2008) www.dni.gov/nic/NIC_2025_project.html (accessed May 13, 2009).

5. Patrick Johnstone, *The Church Is Bigger Than You Think* (Scotland, Christian Focus Publications, 1998).

6. Bryan Nicholson, Global Mapping International, (2009) using data from UNICEF.

7. Bryan Nicholson, Global Mapping International, 2009 using Patrick Johnstone's data prepared for two upcoming publications.

8. Ibid.

9. Wess Stafford, *Too Small to Ignore* (Colorado Springs: WaterBrook Press, 2005), 212.

10. Dan Brewster and Keith White, *Dictionary of Mission Theology*, ed. John Corrie (Downers Grove, IL: InterVarsity Press), 46.

11. Keith White, "A Little Child Shall Lead Them: Rediscovering Children at the Heart of Mission," www.childtheology.org/new/docuploads/A%20little%20child%20will%20lead%20 them.doc (accessed February 21, 2009).

12. Roy Zuck, *Precious in His Sight* (Grand Rapids: Baker, 1996), 18.

13. Ibid., quoted in Frank G. Coleman, *The Romance of Winning Children* (Cleveland: Union Gospel Press, 1967), 9–10.

14. United Nations; data refer to population aged 5–14. Courtesy of Global Mapping International.

15. Jason Mandryk, "State of the Gospel 2006," Joshua Project, http://www.joshuaproject. net/great-commission-powerpoints.php (accessed June 11, 2009).

16. NationMaster, http://www.nationmaster.com/graph/peo_age_str_0_14_yea-age-structure- 0-14-years (accessed February 20, 2009).

17. Glenn Miles and Josephine-Joy Wright, *Celebrating Children* (Carlisle, UK: Paternoster Press, 2003), 130.

18. Dan Brewster, "Themes and Implications of Holistic Child Development Programming in Seminaries" (paper written for Asia Theological Association conference on Leadership in an Age of Crisis, unpublished), 6, 51.

19. Ibid.

20. James E. Katz and Mark Aakhus, eds., *Perpetual Contact: Mobile Communication, Private Talk, Public Performance* (Cambridge, UK: Cambridge University Press, 2002), 138.

21. The World Values Survey is an ongoing academic project by social scientists to assess the state of socio-cultural, moral, religious, and political values of different cultures around the world. The project has produced more than 300 publications in 14 languages.

22. Zuck, *Precious in His Sight*. 202.

23. Dan Brewster, *Children and Childhood in the Bible Workbook*, (Penang, Malaysia: Compassion International, 2008), 26.

24. Ibid. 36.

25. White, "A Little Child Shall Lead Them."

26. Glenn Miles and Josephine-Joy Wright, *Celebrating Children*, 130.

27. Adapted from Bryant Myers, "Transformational Development Course Notes," Fuller Theological Seminary: School of Intercultural Studies, January 2003.

28. Dan Brewster, "The 4/14 Window: Child Ministries and Mission Strategy," *Children in Crisis: A New Commitment*, ed. Phyllis Kilbourn (Monrovia, CA: MARC, 1996).

29. George Barna, *Transforming Your Children into Spiritual Champions* (Ventura, CA: Regal, 2003).

30. Ibid, 58.

31. George Barna, "Research Shows That Spiritual Maturity Process Should Start at a Young Age," (Ventura, California: The Barna Group, November 17, 2003) http://www.barna.org/barna-update/article/5-barna-update/130-research-shows-that-spiritual-maturity-process-should-start-at-a-young-age (accessed June 11, 2009).

32. Jean Piaget, "Stages of Intellectual Development in Children and Teenagers," Child Development Institute, http://www.childdevelopmentinfo.com/development/piaget.shtml (accessed February 17, 2009).

33. John 17:14-18.

34. Samuel P. Huntington and Lawrence E. Harrison, *Culture Matters: How Values Shape Human Progress* (New York: Basic Books, 2000).

35. Lee Kuan Yew, quoted by Fareed Zakaria, "A Conversation with Lee Kuan Yew," *Foreign Affairs*, March–April 1994, 52.

36. Country-based transformation indicators have been prepared by the Joshua Project and are based on more than 100 separate indicators organized by spiritual, humanitarian, and behavioral categories. These are then weighed equally to make up the composite transformational indicator for the country.

37. D. Gordon et al., "Study: Child Poverty in the Developing World." (Bristol, UK: Centre for International Poverty Research, 2003).

38. "Children on the Brink 2004 Factsheet," UNAIDS, USAID, UNICEF, http://www.unicef.org/media/files/COB_2004_fact_sheet.doc (accessed June 11, 2009).

39. Gordon, "Study: Child Poverty."

40. "Teen Challenge Swaziland," Teen Challenge, http://www.childinthemidst.org/xml/ pray. xml?uniqueID=8393 (accessed February 17, 2009).

41. United Nations, "End Poverty 2015: Millennium Development Goals," September 2008, www.un.org/millenniumgoals/2008highlevel/pdf/newsroom/Goal%206%20FINAL.pdf (accessed June 15, 2009).

42. Jennifer Thurman, "House Rejects Africa AIDS/Abstinence Aid," July 2, 2007. http:// cafetheology.org/2007/07/03/house-rejects-africa-aidsabstinence-aid/ (accessed June 15, 2009).

43. Janet Museveni, quoted by Shawn Hendricks, "Ugandan First Lady Honor for Support of Abstinence Promotion." Baptist Press, June 23, 2004, http://www.bpnews.net/bpnews. asp?id=18556 (accessed June 11, 2009).

44. Ibid.

45. Swizen Kyomuhendo et al., *Uganda National Abstinence and Being Faithful Policy and Strategy on Prevention of Transmission of HIV: Draft Policy and Strategy* (Uganda AIDS Commission, November 2004), iv.

46. Thurman, "House Rejects Africa AIDS/Abstinence Aid."

47. D. Gordon, "Study: Child Poverty."

48. Ibid.

49. Dan Brewster and Patrick McDonald, "Children: The Great Omission," Lausanne 2004 Forum, http://www.viva.org/en/articles/great_omission/ great_ omission_booklet.pdf (accessed February 17, 2009).

50. UNICEF, "The State of the World's Children," (2008), 134, http://www.unicef.org/ publications/files/The_State_of_the_Worlds_Children_2008.pdf.

51. World Health Organization, Ibid.

52. George Otis Jr., "International Fellowship of Transformation Partners Definition and Values," Transform World Indonesia 2005 (May 2005).

53. John Rucyahana, The 4/14 Window, e-mail to author, January 24, 2009.

54. Brewster, "Themes and Implications," 6.

55. Oxford Statement for Children at Risk, 1997, produced by Oxford Centre for Mission Studies and Viva Network.

56. Bryant Myers, *Walking with the Poor: Principles and Practices of Transformational Development* (New York: Orbis Books, 1999).

57. Chad Causley, international director for Global Ministries, OneHope, in discussion with author, January 2009.

58. Former members of gangs in El Salvador, in discussion with author, San Salvador, June 2008.

59. William Damon, *Greater Expectations,* (New York: Free Press Paperbacks, 1995), 84.

60. Ibid., 84–85.

61. Ibid., 86.

62. Alister Doyle, "Norway Tops 2005 U.N. Ranking as Best Place to Live," August 26, 2005, http://www.redorbit.com/news/international/221347/norway_tops_2005_un_ranking_as_best_place_to_live/ (accessed June 11, 2009).

63. Arild Stubhaug, *Dagbladet*, June 11, 1998, translated and paraphrased by Hans Thore Lovaas, September 4, 2005.

64. Joseph D'Souza is the international president of the Dalit Freedom Movement and the All India Christian Council, OM India, and chairman of Transform World India 2006, an event in which more than 1,000 servant leaders from India took part. E-mail to author, February 22, 2009.

65. Population statistics for the Dalits remain controversial. According to Joseph D'Souza in an e-mail to the author on February 22, 2009, the best figure is 250 million, which takes into consideration both the scheduled castes and tribes.

66. Udit Raj (Ram Raj) is the national president of the Justice Party and the Confederation of Scheduled Caste/Scheduled Tribe Organizations.

67. Kancha Ilaiah, professor at Osmania University, calls the Christian church to focus on the abolition of untouchability and caste discrimination in India. He has coined the term "spiritual democracy," which means human equality before the Creator. He points out that biblical Christianity provides for a culture of acceptance as equals. Kancha advocates that the Dalits enter the spiritual democratic space available within the biblical tradition of Christianity to discover their true identity and human dignity with accompanying socio-spiritual implications.

68. Joseph D'Souza, e-mail to author, January 11, 2009. For more information, go to www.dalitchild.com or www.dalitnetwork.org.

69. Alex Harris and Brett Harris, *Do Hard Things* (Colorado Springs: Multnomah Books, 2008), 97.

70. Damon, *Greater Expectations,* 128.

71. Lucille Talusan, "Childlike Faith Transforms Indonesian Village," Christian World News, http://www.youtube.com/watch?v=vSlKKHoBXf4 (accessed February 17, 2009).

72. Ibid.

73. Ibid.

74. Ruslan Sangadji, "Road to Eternal Peace: Poso, Central Sulawesi," Planet Mole, December 26, 2007, http://www.planetmole.org/indonesian-news/road-to-eternal-peace-poso-central-sulawesi.html (accessed February 17, 2009).

75. Robert Coles, *The Spiritual Life of Children* (Boston, Houghton Mifflin, 1990).

76. John Robb, e-mail to author, December 16, 2008.

77. Ibid.

78. Leon Morris, *The Gospel According to St. Luke: An Introduction and Commentary* (Grand Rapids, Eerdmans, 1974), 226, quoted in Zuck, *Precious in His Sight.*

79. Dan Brewster, *Child, Church and Mission* (Colorado Springs: Compassion International, 2005), 40.

80. Jaisankar Sarma, director of World Vision Transformation Development International,

international director for Transformation Development, facilitator of Transformation Indicators Task Force for WVI, Personal interview in Washington DC, 25 January 2006.

81. Ibid.

82. Malcolm Webber, "The ConneXions Model," adapted with permission of Malcolm Webber, LeaderSource SGA. For the complete models, see Healthy Leaders: SpiritBuilt Leadership No. 2, and Building Leaders: SpiritBuilt Leadership No. 4, www.leadersource. org and www.leadershipletters.com.

83. James E. Loder, *The Transforming Moment* (Colorado Springs, Helmers & Howard, 1989), back cover.